WOMEN'S CHOICES, MIDWIFE VOICES

what does it mean to be radical?

Lynn R S Genevieve

Garmoran Publishing

All profits from the sale of this book will be donated to the Association of Radical Midwives.
Registered charity no: 10660525

ISBN-: 9781913510060
eISBN-: 9781913510077

Cover design by: Willow Findlay

For Carol, 'little' Nicky, Gina,Carrie and 'big' Nicky. You may not be part of ARM, but you are at heart the most radical of midwives - you have all supported women's choices, and you have always supported me. Thank you.

You are a midwife, assisting at someone else's birth. Do good without show or fuss. Facilitate what is happening rather than what you think ought to be happening. If you must take the lead, lead so that the mother is helped, yet still free and in charge. When the baby is born, the mother will rightly say, 'We did it ourselves!'

TAO TE CHING (THE WAY)

CONTENTS

FOREWORD

I felt so honoured when Lynn asked me to write a foreword to her midwifery memoire, her time as a midwife which now feels as if it was the golden age of midwifery. Midwives' voices, strengthened by feminism and radical midwifery, greatly multiplied women's choices in childbirth – including the ability to say, "No thanks, I don't want that". (I am reminded of a tale told of one of my sisters who didn't want help with tying her school tie – "I'll do it myself and go with it wrong," - because choice means accepting responsibility for the consequences of those choices.) No longer did we have to accept a patriarchy which forced unwanted medical management of birth upon us for our own good. Now the person with ultimate responsibility for the baby could make the decisions. The very existence of independent midwifery (IMs) increased choice for all, it provided a real alternative, IMs showed the NHS how it could (and should) be done. When my local hospital was "too busy" even to talk to a term+10 mother or her partner on the phone, Ishbel, the Association of Radical Midwives (ARM), Ros and independent midwifery saved the day and I've been a member of ARM ever since.

Though not myself a midwife, I am, nevertheless, a full member of the Association of Radical Midwives. My membership status reflects ARM's philosophy that mothers are seen as full and equal partners in birth. There is no hierarchy, no expert midwife and ignorant mother, only women working together in harmony to enable babies to have the best birth possible in whatever circumstances the mother finds herself in.

Lynn invited contributions from twelve midwives. It was fun to have a dozen puzzles to solve, would I recognise my friends by what it meant to them to be radical? Yes, most of the time I could. What a delight it was and great to meet so many old friends again, particularly after eighteen months of virtual lockdown.

The foreword to another book on Radical Midwifery was written by Mary Cronk to celebrate ARM's 21st birthday in 1997. Mary taught midwives how to be radical, how to bend the system when quaking at the knees; by dropping the episiotomy scissors - thus rendering them non-sterile; by inviting the consultant to come in and administer an enema to 'his' woman, because Mary wasn't going to be doing it (he didn't). Small acts of research-based anarchy ensured that the midwifery profession did not become a victim of the NHS reorganisation of 1974 when the administrative responsibility for all birth was transferred wholesale to the NHS. Before then, the district midwife had been employed by the local authority and had her own 'patch'.

Reorganisation placed midwives under hospital management which risked institutionalised birth under medical control. It is no coincidence that ARM was founded only two years later. The writing was on the wall; there was a real danger that midwives would become obstetric nurses, under the control of doctors and nursing officers. Hospital birth controls the midwife as much as it does the mother, midwives had to become radical to resist becoming medicalised themselves.

The erroneous link with nursing was reinforced and strengthened when the Central Midwives Board was subsumed into the UKCC – the UK Central Council for Nursing, Midwifery and Health Visiting renamed the Nursing and Midwifery Council (NMC) in 2001. But ARM fought back, managing at least to make sure there was a statutory midwifery committee.

There were however two places where midwives could – and still can - practise as real midwives; the woman's own home and midwifery units, some of which had evolved from the old maternity homes or GP units, and some of which were newly built following the Birthplace Study of 2011 which identified free-standing midwifery units, birth centres, as the safest places for 'low risk' women and their babies (home was safest for all women, and for all but first born babies). Another way of looking at this is to say that choosing to labour in hospital increases risk for women and their babies; hospital is safe only because there is an operating theatre to 'rescue' women from mismanaged labour and a special care baby unit to cater for obstetric accidents. Both overused today.

Of course, safe out of hospital birth also depends upon ready access to obstetric back up when needed - the real skill in midwifery is knowing when to seek more help. Lynn gives a few instances from her practice. Would that all midwives needing to transfer care could follow her professional lead in managing the process – but as she points out, self-employment was an advantage, her contract was with her client not the hospital management.

Today there is an emphasis on teamwork. But for out-of-hospital birth under autonomous midwives, it is the security of knowing that there is a team in the background, ambulance, hospital, obstetrician, that makes birth safe. In hospital there is always the risk that the senior person (i.e., the best paid) will take it upon themselves to be the team leader. But even if the surgical or instrumental skills of an obstetrician are required, the need for the midwife is ongoing and persists after that intervention. A mother needing obstetric help has even more need of someone to be alongside her to be 'with woman', to protect her and her baby from unnecessary trauma, to see her through the process and to pick up the pieces and to guide her into confident motherhood. The joy of independent midwifery is that the relationship can continue to the next baby and the next.

Radical midwives give mothers the freedom to be radical themselves, to stand up and embrace responsibility for their birth, their body, their children. Radical midwives make strong mothers. Radical midwifery is the only way to keep the patriarchy out of birth. It remains our hope for the future. We must continue our fight to retain home birth and midwife led birth centres and shout to ensure that women's voices are still heard and respected.

Margaret Jowitt

PREFACE

By presenting this book as 'a living archive', the transcribed voices and Coven essays will reflect the range of opinion of individuals without censure. Any articles shared have been attributed to the authors and commentary throughout the work is of my own thinking. The text and contributions may not reflect the views of the Association of Radical Midwives. You will see from the varied responses to the question 'what does it mean to you, to be radical?' that answers show diverse opinions. As ARM is a community of like-minded midwives and those interested in childbirth that grew out of the post second wave feminist era, the language throughout this text will express many points of view and habits.

A Living Archive

This publication reflects the views of the membership of the Association of Radical Midwives (ARM) as well as me. It became a hybrid memoir with many personal accounts as well as a living archive capturing the organisation 'warts and all'. (Presaging a constant theme in the book of 'midwives as witches', I'm sure that radical midwives won't mind a few warts...).

Rhodes (2014) defines the documentation of social movements as:

A "living archive" is a collection of materials presented in a way that allows for the expression, exhibition, documentation and preservation of a sentiment or movement in a particular community".

ARM was my touchstone for all midwifery philosophy and political enquiry during my years as a practicing midwife. The membership although comparatively small, made up for their size through committed engagement in national and international midwifery discussions and decision making, representing the UK in the ICM (International Confederation of Midwives) conferences world-wide, and contributing to every government debate and consultation involving midwifery and birth in the UK that was possible. Although some perceived ARM's ideals as minority ones, our input came to be recognised as well informed and innovative, gaining support widely from the public (women and families) as well as professionals. ARM's roots were in feminism, but I believe that they carved out a unique view of birth and midwifery care, that supported the best of the past, with the most appropriate of the modern era. ARM reflected and took forward important features of the world of birth from the point of view of both women and professionals.

Women's Choices: Midwife Voices grew out the idea of 'verbatim theatre' where peoples' words are transcribed and then turned into authentic plays. I was intrigued with the idea of using real 'voices' to bring authenticity and asked the membership only one question - 'What does it mean to you to be radical?' Their responses were recorded at online meetings.

Despite my overriding belief that the midwives' stories should be central, I have found that for midwives to share their experiences, it has sometimes meant sharing birth stories. I have given in gracefully myself, scattering the book with some of the births I attended professionally. Whilst I insist that this is not a piece of research and that I try very hard not to analyse others' words, I do explore my own feelings on these themes throughout the text, as well as in the birth stories themselves.

Themes

Reading the transcripts of the ARM members talking about 'being radical' and invited contributors' considerations on the question - 'what does it mean to you, to be radical?' - keywords have stood out. I have sifted these words into a limited group of themes, purely for the organisation of the book. The invited contributors' (the Coven) responses are shared as complete, unedited, and attributed to the authors. The meetings transcripts are sampled and anonymous, but I have committed to including every single participant. The contributors' answers range from a simple, short paragraph, to a complete essay; I have neither directed nor asked for changes or edits.

The general areas I identified are:

1. Roots (nurture and nourish)
2. Normality (natural)
3. Feminism (politics and patriarchy)
4. Choice (advocacy and support)
5. Power (empowerment)
6. Vocation (passion and purpose)
7. Knowledge (questioning and information)
8. Witch hunts
9. Trust (authenticity)
10. Inclusivity (diversity).

Selected birth stories from my years in practice demonstrate some of the areas discussed to put these themes in context. In these memoir snippets, I can illustrate in further detail how these themes are radical, adding linking commentary and appropriate reprinted articles from ARM's magazine 'Midwifery Matters'.

INTRODUCTION

The Tao Te Ching quote 'You are a Midwife' (epigraph in front pages), written so long ago, encapsulates the very essence of a midwife. To be a skilful midwife today, to uphold this ancient, tried and tested culture of good practice, means that a midwife must be radical, in my opinion. I am a midwife (retired) and proud to be able to say that I was a radical midwife during my years of practice. Midwifery, (I hazard a guess that it was the second oldest profession if prostitution is deemed the first, they would have needed midwives) is a profession that has a history steeped in mistrust and controversy. From the Bible to the witch hunts of the medieval era, through Patriarchal societies and the rise of the medical profession, midwives have been pursued and prosecuted to the point in the twentieth century when, at least in the west, they were almost stamped out (Donnison 1988, Ehrenreich & English 2010). Most of this troubled history it is proposed, can be explained by what some call herstory (Reed 2021) the attempt to silence and subjugate women, an ongoing campaign encapsulated in the regular 'waves' of feminism.

The Birth of a Coven

Throughout my years as a midwife, a common trope was repeatedly applied to midwives who challenged the system - a 'witch'. These midwives would often find themselves at odds with employers (NHS) or the regulatory body the Nursing & Midwifery Council (NMC). Certain midwives, those working independently of the NHS (as I did), those not following hospital policies or those who openly challenged the 'powers that be' even when advocating for women, would find themselves subject to investigations, suspensions, or bullying. Somewhere along the line, the term 'witch hunt' was adopted as an all-encompassing term to describe these situations when kind and compassionate midwives, supporting women's choices were singled out and their practice scrutinised.

I am not talking here about the right and proper process of investigating incidents and poor outcomes at birth, this is part and process of the life of those working in maternity care - doctors, obstetricians and paediatricians are just as vulnerable to close inspection. However, when midwives' adverse outcomes are focused upon, if they have been vocal in their philosophy of midwifery as different (and here, I would emphasise 'radical') then it is these individuals that have been labelled as 'dangerous' and hounded out of the profession.

Article

A Global Witch-Hunt

Marsden Wagner has been involved in 20 cases of alleged professional misconduct over the last ten years. His editorial in The Lancet says that:

"There is a global witch-hunt in progress...the investigation of health professionals in many countries to accuse them of dangerous maternity practices. This witch-hunt is part of a global struggle for control of maternity services, the key underlying issues being money, power, sex, and choice."

He pulls out common features of the cases he has been involved in. These include:

• imbalanced sex ratio - 70% were midwives and 85% were women;

• at least some of their practice is not mainstream - of the twenty accused, 15 practised home births, three practised in alternative birth centres, and two were doctors in hospital practice.

• All of the midwives were in independent practice (despite the fact that unorthodox providers are rarely sued by parents whereas 70% of USA and UK obstetricians have been sued at least once).

• Evidence gathering - In most cases, the doctors notify the legal authorities only after a perinatal death. One death, even if not preventable and not the result of any mistake, suddenly negates years of impeccable statistics.

• Consequences to the individual - If the accused loses, that often means losing the possibility, at least temporarily, of continuing to practise.

• Impact on other health professionals - Midwives in that country feel threatened in their independent practice. Doctors are afraid to support midwives or to go along with the wishes of their patients when the requests are outside mainstream policy – e.g. water births.

• Loss of choice for women.

On the other hand, investigation of independent midwives and unorthodox doctors can sometimes have the opposite effect, leading to solidarity among midwives and between midwives and unorthodox doctors, and women, irrespective of whether the accused wins or loses.

He continues:

"The witch-hunt is part of a global struggle for control of maternity systems and there are several key issues, one of which is economic.

"As birth rates fall, the competition for pregnant patients increases, especially in countries largely reliant on private medical care; and as more and more countries move towards pluralistic health care systems with private practice, maternity care becomes more competitive. However, in the face of increasingly limited economic resources, governments and insurance companies are becoming more and more concerned with the waste associated with high-technology, high-intervention obstetrics. It is much more difficult for obstetricians to defend this expensive type of practice when midwives and a few doctors are meanwhile showing that a much less expensive type of maternity care is equally safe...The witch-hunt is an attempt to display lack of safety among the competitors.

"...A second issue is the control of maternity services. Until recently, government regulations in most countries have given doctors a monopoly in providing health services. But this monopoly can easily be abused, especially behind closed doors. The issue becomes one of peer control versus accountability to the public.

"Fortunately the pendulum is swinging, at least in some places, with the coming of quality assurance systems that include public accountability of health care and health care professionals. Maternity services are in the forefront of the controversy over peer control and public accountability because birth, like death, is a deeply personal social and family event and does not fit the doctors' disease model. So today the medical monopoly of maternity services is coming into question and the witch-hunt is one means of reasserting the orthodox doctor's control. Choice and freedom for health care consumers are at issue here. In the USA and UK, consumers of health care have been asserting themselves for some time. The claim is made that the obstetrician must protect the best interest of the fetus by overriding any woman's choice not approved by orthodox obstetricians. As pluralistic health care systems increase in Europe, so will consumer choice; the witch¬ hunt is one way of limiting that freedom of choice.

"Choice and freedom for healthcare providers are also at stake here...It is no coincidence that 90% of the accused in my sample were involved in home birth or alternative birth centres. It is important to distinguish between the quality assurance function and the witch-hunt function so that the courts are not inappropriately used for professional gain. When making that distinction in a particular case, think about who might gain from a successful prosecution; is the evidence brought against the accused scientifically based? Whilst tribunals may have a declared function to weed out true incompetence and protect the public in the cases I describe the real function was to punish deviant professional behaviour that could threaten the income, practice style, prestige, and power of mainstream doctors.

"...Another issue is the two-hundred-year-old struggle of doctors to control midwifery. It is no coincidence that 70% of the accused in my sample are midwives, all in independent practice where they are not under the immediate control of doctors. Fear of being investigated by authorities is a strong deterrent to independent midwives.

"Solutions begin with increasing the public's awareness of the witch-hunt and its basis in political not medical issues.

"There should be no closed doors in health policy making, in health service delivery, or when the behaviour of health professionals is being judged. The evaluation of professional behaviour must be based on deviations from practice based on scientific evidence rather than on deviations from peer-controlled opinions of what constitutes good practice?'

The Lancet - vol 346
Midwifery Matters 100 - Spring 2004

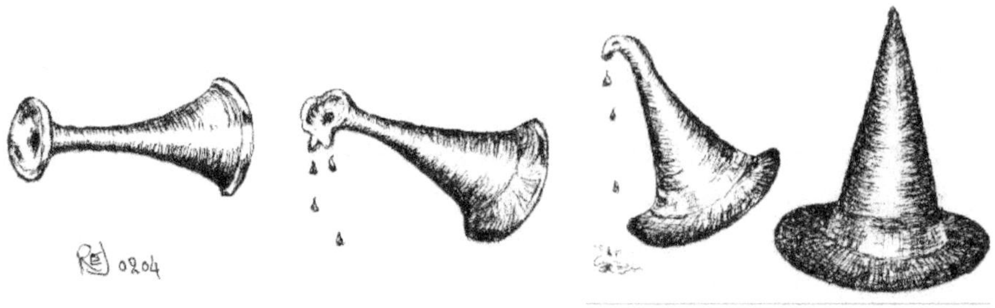

ROOTS

Coven contributor

'What does it mean to you, to be radical?"
I think that often to identify as a radical midwife is to be seen as someone who is militant or someone who rejects everything about modern midwifery. Radicalism is now seen as a concept associated with extremism. Socially I think this is the case as the global understanding of the word has shifted over time. However, I think it is also easier to externalise and reject something that can cause inner challenges, raising questions about individual identity and what it means to be a midwife.

However, that is not what being radical means to me. For me being radical is about staying true to the essence of something. That essence is within, it is cellular, spiritual, and energetic. It is also social in that I think to nurture it you need to be connected with people that recognise that essence too. I try to focus on the essence of or the root of midwifery when I wish to ground myself in my identity as a midwife and be true to myself and what I see as important in my life and in my way of being. They are interconnected and not separate. It is a radical action to peel back the layers of midwifery practice and reconnect to that root.

Connection is central to being radical, but connection is multidimensional for me. I am connected to the generations of midwives that went before me, so history is important in grounding my concept of radicalism. That history lets me see what was radical and what was not, it helps me be the weed that grows up through the cracks in the pavement.

Connection is also about the people around me. It is radical to be with women, it is radical to be with birthing people, it is radical to be with other midwives and it is radical to forge those connections with other people in the birthing world – however they are in that world. If there is connection and understanding then that is radical. Sometimes being radical is holding the torch and leading the way. The ARM has done that in many ways and it is wonderful to connect into that passion and sit with powerful women and feel connection. Sometimes being radical is holding being a tiny light in the dark trying to be the connection.'

Nessa McHugh

The Coven

As well as the verbatim transcripts of midwives' voices answering the question: "What does it mean to you to be radical?" I invited a particular dozen midwives that I knew and had regard for to also answer this question, with a choice to either have a verbatim transcription as per the other voices, or in a written, perhaps more considered form. In counting myself as an additional member answering the question, I had thirteen names, the number used in a witches' coven, all voices that I had carefully curated.

But there are three names missing from my Coven. Three midwives that had been mentors and friends for many years who are no longer alive to answer the question, what does it mean to you to be radical? All midwives who undoubtedly as members of ARM, I believe would have agreed to be part of the coven. I toyed with the idea of simply including them as they all had previously published work that reflected their 'radical' credentials, however, I did not feel comfortable doing this without their permission. Consent in midwifery is for me paramount, therefore without their consent for inclusion, I could not proceed. But I would like to share their names and a small taste of their personalities. It's fair to say, all three were kind, compassionate but feisty women, passionate about birth and midwifery, a massive loss to many personally, and the ARM and maternity world is the poorer for their passing.

Mary Cronk MBE (1932 - 2018)

It would be easy to write an entire book about Mary, and indeed, I hope that one day, someone does, but Mary, for me, really was the great Matriarch of ARM and midwifery. The book 'Community Midwifery' (1989) that she co-wrote (with Caroline Flint, another of my Coven) was the first book I read about midwifery and sealed my decision to one day train as a midwife.

I was thrilled to meet Mary at an ARM national meeting in the early 1990's. We were both regulars to these meetings held all over the country, and I would sit in rapt attention, soaking up every word she uttered. Years later, when Mary and I were friends and midwifery colleagues, I recall watching other student midwives sat at her feet with the same awe etched on their faces that must have been visible in my own at those early meetings. Mary was enormously experienced and wise, truly, her snippets of 'lore' are legendary (found on the internet variously as 'assertiveness phrases', 'famous sayings', 'famous quotes', 'words of wisdom' or 'Mary Cronk's phrasebook').

Mary was also generous with her time and knowledge; I was one of many whom she mentored, but she was a dear friend. In her last years, I was living 600 miles away in Scotland, Mary's homeland, so could not visit regularly as I used to. For more than three years we corresponded, and our friendship deepened. When she died in 2018, I attended her funeral, the family kindly sharing their private grief to allow the many people whose lives Mary had touched, to come together and pay tribute; it was like a 'who's who' of the midwifery profession. I owed much of my midwifery skill and knowledge to this incredible woman.

Tricia Anderson (1961 - 2007)

Tricia was hugely influential on my midwifery career. I saw her as inhabiting the sweetest spot; she was both a teacher (senior lecturer at Bournemouth University) and an independent midwife (IM). Tricia more than anyone else I ever met, managed to combine academia with clinical practise in such a way as to not diminish either. Tricia was the epitome of a midwife who inhabited that space of the art and science of birth. She was able to take all that was great about traditional midwifery care and weave it into modern practice in a way that met women's needs completely.

The first time I met Tricia was at a midwifery conference as a student midwife. I tentatively sidled up to her to cheerily share my aspirations to be an IM just like her. "Why on earth would you want to be an independent midwife?" The reply that floored me. As I stammered an inadequate response, she listed the many and real difficulties of midwifery practice outside of the NHS... then smiled. I relaxed and continued in a more confident reply at my need to serve women through relationship, what is known as 'continuity of carer', not commonplace in the UK in the 1990's despite being a traditional model of care (it is now government policy). I suspect it was a test and I passed. Tricia went on to be a valued support and friend when my life as an IM became littered with those difficulties that she had raised with me that day.

Again, when Tricia died, her family generously shared her funeral service with a multitude of midwives and mothers - incidentally, the same location as Mary went on to choose for her final resting place - a natural burial ground in Dorset. A year after Tricia's death, I attended a conference held in her honour as so many people wished to celebrate her life and achievements where she was awarded with a posthumous PhD.

Clare Fisher (1963 - 2018)

Clare was a 'one off' - I think that's the term to use. More passionate about birth and women's autonomy than anyone I have ever met, she sacrificed much to her beliefs and taught me so much about 'love'. Because Clare was committed to supporting women's choices, she was regularly at odds with her local NHS senior midwifery personnel. She lived in an area of the UK that was very rural, and appeared to have extreme, fixed policies on what women 'could or could not' do - as if the NHS had any authority over female agency. Clare advocated for women in home birth situations, typical scenarios that IMs like us came up against regularly where women had fallen out with the local NHS over plans for birth. This made Clare a target for those determined to hunt such autonomous and strong midwives, a true witch hunt in every sense. Clare was to spend more than fifteen years of her life battling against NHS management, Supervision of Midwifery and the NMC (Nursing and Midwifery Council), to clear her name - and she did. She had endured case after case of investigation, was accused of many untrue acts and omissions, and eventually was awarded compensation by the Ombudsman. But those years took their toll, and her health suffered. In the year she was to have retired from midwifery, only in her 50s, Clare died quite suddenly.

I remember the call vividly. I happened to be on a visit in the south of England from my home in Scotland. I answered my phone,

"Hi Clare, how are you?" I was aware that she had been having some medical tests.

"I'm dying Lynn...". What on earth do you say to that? Clare was an experienced nurse; she knew the score. "It's the liver, Lynn. It's weeks, not months." She then proceeded to invite me to her wedding that Friday (this was Monday) in Wales. I was both devastated and honoured that she was not only inviting me to the wedding, but that she wanted me as a witness. Clare's family at that time were mostly far flung - adult children in France, America, and Australia - and three others still at school and at home in Wales. Her darling partner was Roo, together with Clare for more than thirty years, but they had never married. This is how amazing this family is - they arranged a wedding in days, all flew in from around the world, and I have to say it was the most beautiful and meaningful wedding I have ever attended. Incidentally, the other witness that day was another of the Coven, Paul. We witches clearly stick together.

Clare was sadly right. Only a few weeks later, Roo called to say that she'd died, at home with family around her - I'd spoken to her only days before. Clare was larger than life - truly. She never deserved what she endured from those witch hunts.

Coven contributor

Mary Cronk and I had a challenging relationship as she decided she was going to be my mentor. She would regularly call me with advice, praise and criticism. I learnt so much from her and was proud to call her my friend. She once contacted me in my role as a SOM [supervisor of midwives] when I was the Director of Maternity Services at the West London Hospital.

She wanted to bring one of her women into our labour ward. The woman had made good progress in labour and her cervix was fully dilated. However, she had stopped contracting and went to sleep for several hours. Mary had continued to monitor the FHR [foetal heart rate] and the health of the mother and was happy that neither were at risk. When the mother eventually awoke and her contractions didn't return, Mary thought it was necessary to bring her into hospital.

Mary and mother arrived in our labour ward and I went to talk with them. The mother and unborn baby were both fine and Mary wanted her to have some time to adjust to being in hospital. After a very short while there was an onset of contractions and fairly rapidly, the baby was born safe and well.

The second stage of labour was over fifteen hours. It showed me that while this was not what most if not all, would consider to be 'normal', it was.

This woman had the right midwife, with the right skills, knowledge, and confidence to give birth without intervention. Mary had brought her into hospital as she felt this was safer given the length of labour but continued to support the mother to achieve a normal birth. She was a real loss to our profession.

Tricia Anderson was also a very much-loved colleague. And I still think she was the brightest midwife I had ever met.

Claire Fisher however, was of a completely different order of 'Midwife'. She was tough and amazing. I first met her when she was fighting to exonerate herself and refute allegations made against her by a midwifery manager who was not only a bully, but a seriously vindictive bitch.

Claire's enemies became mine and I tried to support her and offer advice i.e., don't parade naked with placards outside the NMC building, when and where I could. I was honoured when asked to be one of her witnesses when she finally married Roo, and as you know she died shortly after.

The many, many women from the Valleys and Village who came to her wedding and wept for their loss when she died, was testimony of how great a midwife she was.

As I get older and fall into obscurity I miss them all.

(Part 1)

Professor Paul Lewis OBE

Midwife – meaning *with woman*

Today, women's voices as mothers, their experiences of pregnancy, giving birth and afterwards are becoming well documented, but midwives, who are *with* them on this journey, are largely silent. That is, midwives support, advocate, share these experiences, but most often regarding the women themselves as the focus, amplifying the woman's view. Radical midwives by their very nature, tend to remain in the background, their voices rarely heard except when supporting women directly, listening being far more important to our role than action. The only medical instrument specifically associated with a midwife is a Pinard's stethoscope (mostly referred to as a Pinard today), a listening device (to hear the foetal heart (FH) when in utero), traditionally made of wood. In modern maternity care it is rarely seen as technology dominates, but as a radical midwife, I used it with all my clients. The Pinards' decline mirrors the demise of midwife autonomy.

Article

Me and My Pinard's
by Mary Cronk

THIS ARTICLE has been in my head for some time. I actually didn't believe that there were midwives qualifying who had never heard a fetal heart, didn't know what it sounded like, and didn't know the provenance of the Pinard's stethoscope. Then I met several students who asked me to teach them how to use it and then I realised that an article like this might be useful.

'Pinard's' have a capital P as it is named after a Dr. Pinard, a Frenchman who produced it sometime in the mid 19th century. It was widely used for auscultation in medical practice until the binaural stethoscope was invented.

Before I became a midwife I trained as a nurse at Glasgow Royal Infirmary. In those days medical practitioners had little or no technology other than x-rays to assist them in diagnosis and they relied almost totally upon clinical observation. A venerable Honorary Cardiac Physician, when he did his Ward Round insisted on a tray being carried by the senior staff nurse who followed Sister who followed Sir. On this tray were laid out Sir's equipment: various hammers, head mirror, etc. and three different designs of Pinard 's stethoscopes. He used these if he wished to confirm what he was hearing with that new- fangled piece of equipment - the binaural stethoscope. He also insisted that the students listen with it, they did this with varying degrees of hidden sniggering, scepticism and sneering.

Listening to the fetal heart

A careful palpation saves lots of time. The aim is to hear the fetal heart through the fetal back. Thus, the bell end of the instrument is positioned over the place on the maternal abdomen under which it is felt that the fetal back lies, remember the lungs are not inflated and the fetal heart can be heard clearly through the back. If the position seems to be LOA, position the wide end of the Pinard's about halfway between the umbilicus and the symphysis pubis and about two inches to the left. If the head is engaged move it down a bit. Apply your ear to the flat end; you will need to apply gentle pressure and indent the abdomen nearly a centimetre, depending on the thickness of the abdominal wall. Take your hand away from the Pinard's, listen -and keep listening.

You are listening for a sound that is in the distance and sounds like a watch ticking under a pillow, but of course faster than a ticking watch. If you have an old fashioned watch that ticks, try it (borrow one from your grandpa). Often at first it feels more Ike a vibration than a sound. If you hear a slow 'shooching' noise you are probably hearing the maternal vessels supplying the uterus. Feel the maternal pulse at the same time and if it coincides with the 'shooching' you are hearing the uterine vessels. The technical name for that is a 'uterine souffle' -don't ask me why.

If after careful listening you really can't hear a thing, repeat the palpation and try on the right. If you still can't hear anything that could conceivably be the fetal heart, consider whether the fetus could be in an OP position. If so, you may be able to hear nearer the midline, in which case, you will be hearing the fetal heart through the anterior fetal chest wall. Alternatively, try placing the Pinard 's on the maternal flank i.e., at the side where the mother's waist would have been if she still had one!

You may have to practise and practise, but once you can hear it you have acquired an invaluable skill. If the baby is presenting by the breech, you may be able to hear it better above the umbilicus.

Those of us who worked before ultrasound, often used the place where the fetal heart could be heard most clearly to help us to assess the position and presentation of the fetus. I can rarely hear a fetal heart much before 26 weeks, and if I don't hear it until 30 weeks so what?

Counting

Having managed to find the fetal heart, don't try and count it until your ear is 'tuned' and you have listened to several fetal hearts and feel confident. Use a watch with a decent second hand. I use a digital watch, but many of my colleagues prefer a sweep second hand. Wait until the second hand is at one of the quarters and start counting. Count for 15 secs and multiply by four i.e., 35 beats in 15 secs= 140 bpm. Listen for four quarters of a minute, not necessarily consecutively.

Once you have mastered this, try counting each 5-second interval separately - it should not always be the same. In one 5-sec interval you may hear 10beats (120bpm) then you may hear 14 (168bpm) or 12 (144 bpm). You may even hear an occasional 15 (180bpm). This is how one assesses the beat-to-beat variations. If you find you are consistently hearing exactly the same number of beats every 5 seconds, then there is not much beat-to-beat variation and the little darling's probably asleep. Listen again 15 minutes later.

Advantages and disadvantages

You are hearing this baby's heart beating with your own ears. You are not hearing the ultrasound Doppler effect converted by technology back into sound. What you are hearing is direct; it is not computed or averaged by a hand- held Doppler or a CTG. I am confident that I can nearly always hear a problem before it is picked up on a CTG.

Several of my clients do not wish any ultrasound to be used, unless there is a clear indication, and I am glad that I have retained the skill of using a Pinard's. Having said that, we are encouraged to auscultate much more often these days, and a hand-held Doppler does make life much easier if the woman is on all-fours.

Water

If one is attending a woman who is labouring in a pool and does not wish ultrasound to be used, the long Pinard's (12") enables the fetal heart to be auscultated when the woman is submerged. She does need to raise her abdomen out of the water to apply the end of the long Pinard's, then she can submerge again keeping a seal between the end of the Pinard 's and the abdomen, put your ear to the flat end and if you are in the right place, you will hear the fetal heart.

Fetoscope

I have recently bought a new toy. It is an American fetoscope and I am learning to use it.

I think that, when I am a bit more experienced in its use, I will find that I can hear the fetal heart as clearly as with my Pinard's and, of course, the woman can be in any position she wants.

Midwifery Matters 94 - Autumn 2002

A Birth Story

Becky had two children already, both LSCSs (lower segment caesarean sections), but with the added complication of being Rhesus negative and iso-immunized during her first pregnancy, sometimes called Rhesus disease. (This occurs when a Rhesus negative woman carries a Rhesus positive baby and can be a progressive disease becoming more serious with each pregnancy.) She'd miscarried several times, her last quite late at around eighteen weeks. I was sharing care with specialists in haemolytic disease, but Becky really wanted a normal vaginal birth at home. Her first child had been very jaundiced, her second had required transfusions, she was holding out for a Rhesus negative baby this time which would not be affected. (See Wickham 2021 for more information.)

Becky was a bit of a boffin, a scientist by profession, and duly found out about new research in the private sector that could discern the foetal blood group and more importantly, Rhesus factor from maternal blood sample. (This is a much more freely available test these days.) The usual route, at that time, to have CVS (Chorionic Villus Sampling) or amniocentesis, with a risk of miscarriage, she considered was too risky for her. The blood sample however, was able to confirm that this baby was Rhesus negative, but as the test was so experimental, she continued to have antibody tests throughout the pregnancy. Becky knew her own mind, was certain of how she wanted the birth to go, and just to top things off, she didn't want me to use technology (a sonic aid) to listen to the foetal heart - only a Pinard. Personally, I love using a Pinard, used it regularly, was very confident in what I could and couldn't discern with it and was happy to agree to its use.

Becky got her wish of a trouble-free pregnancy, the tentative confirmation that the baby was in fact Rhesus negative initially was borne out as all antibody tests remained negative throughout this pregnancy. So, in the end, it was just like any other VBAC (Vaginal Birth After Caesarean) situation - just the underlying concerns about going into labour at term and spontaneously. She did and I used only my trusty Pinard throughout the labour, agreeing to use it without words, just a touch to infer a need to listen - Becky understood that I needed to keep close tabs on the FH and her pulse, but wanted a quiet and natural home birth. Not even her husband or children were present. I've had quite a few births like this... just women. All was well, so just like other VBAC situations, it was a confirmation that women's intuition can be trusted, as far as I am concerned.

Coven contributor (recorded at an ARM online meeting)

"I'm always better when it comes spontaneously. I don't like writ-

ing things. I'm very critical. I don't think I write in sentences, but I can speak in them - a lot of life stuff – I'm not an academic. Okay, so radical for me in my career as an NHS midwife, and latterly as an independent midwife has been about reclaiming the origins of midwifery - going back to our midwifery roots of celebrating, of power in what we can do as midwives really. Yeah, 'cause in everyday life I'm not a radical, I keep my head down, I toe the party line on lots. Well, I'm a born sceptic, so perhaps I don't toe the party line. But I'm not out there making a big song and dance about anything, so I wouldn't pass myself off as particularly radical in everyday life, but in midwifery, because it is so, so important, yes - I class myself as a radical midwife. I think I'll leave it there, Lynn."

Joy Horner

NORMALITY

Midwife Voice

N – long standing midwife member of ARM - *'...I think I've always been a midwife even as a child, because I am the eldest of four and my auntie lived two doors, two houses down, had seven children, so she was always either pregnant or breastfeeding. So that was the environment that I grew up in. And then I was present at my mother's last birth, and it was also part of me, if you know what I mean, so normal to be involved in breastfeeding or child rearing or looking after kids, and I wanted to be a midwife. Then I had my children both normally. One in a birth centre and the other one at home. Then, didn't think even anything of that. It was not any sort of radical feminist... any... it was just that's what you did. And then I went and decided... they were old enough... I went to be a direct entry midwife, in a small local northern hospital, where really, everything was quite normal because the midwives there were very... quite old really, and it was this new-fangled midwifery was just coming on board. And so I was part of the team, and it was a sisterhood. It was lovely, it was absolutely lovely to be there, and it was so normal. I kind of drifted along being normal...'*

Below is an editorial by Margaret Jowitt (author of the forward of this book) written during the almost twenty years she was editor of Midwifery Matters.

Article

Editorial - Too Radical?

IN THE WINTER 2001 ISSUE we invited readers to tell us what they thought about the magazine and on the whole the response was reassuring. There was, however, one reply from a reader who feels that the views expressed in the magazine, particularly those of the editor, are not representative of midwives and members of ARM. I am aware that ARM's views are not shared by all midwives, after all why call oneself radical if one shares the majority view? But until now I have been fairly confident that Midwifery Matters reflects the views of most ARM members most of the time. I would hope to hear any adverse comments at ARM National Meetings which I attend regularly, but most are favourable and I hope this is because most members are happy with the magazine more or less how it is. If you are ever upset with anything in the magazine please write a letter for publication. Progress thrives on debate and this magazine should be a forum for all members.

Midwifery Matters is written largely by ARM members and articles are always welcome from any member. Apart from the editorials, I usually write little myself; over the six years since I became editor, an average of one article a year, usually when little else has come in and I have felt the magazine would be rather thin without an extra contribution.

It was very difficult preparing this present issue for publication. Self-doubt was creeping in. A phone call from an ARM student member who was active on the email discussion group 'ukmidwifery' got me wondering whether perhaps ARM is too radical. She has unsubscribed from that list for her remaining time as a student because she feels she must keep her head down; subscribing to the list makes her feel too 'bolshie' which threatens her studies.

So, yes, being too radical can make it difficult to function in the outside world, the 'real world' of being a student midwife, and, I suspect, the 'real world' of NHS midwifery. But does this mean that we should water down the message of radical midwifery? I am inclined to think that for as long as there is a need to 'keep one's head down' in certain environments, there will also be a need for ARM. And I return to an old theme; if some midwives find it difficult to function in their true role of being 'with women' in some environments, then how much harder must it be for the women expected to give birth there? As long as the caesarean section rate continues to climb, as long as midwives continue to leave the profession, unable to tolerate their working conditions any more, a radical midwifery forum will be needed. In some ways the need has been never greater. We can no longer hide behind the fiction that the problem is one of varying philosophies of birth. If it did nothing else, Changing Childbirth did endorse ARM 's philosophy of birth, but the politics of allowing such a climate in the NHS have proved intractable in some areas. I admit I find myself wondering whether more would have been achieved had the Conservatives remained in power. Perhaps we would now have a voucher system which would have enabled women to vote with their feet.

The unhappy reader mistakenly assumed that ARM was an organisation for midwives alone, but it is not. The real need for the maternity services is for everyone to work together in partnership; mother, midwife, obstetrician working towards good safe births for the next generation.

I used to feel that ARM's very name was perhaps wrong - it does have overtones of far, left feminism and anarchy, perhaps it is even dated? But no longer. ARM has come of age in that it is seen in establishment circles as a force for the good in the maternity services. The National Institute for Clinical Excellence sees ARM 's as a useful voice in the maternity services. Our message is not clouded by trade union politics. I feel that we are accepted for what we are, mostly women - midwives and a few mothers - who feel passionately about woman and baby centred maternity care. ARM works with women towards a better maternity service.

ARM fulfils a role that is desperately needed in the current climate and even though there are now more midwifery journals: The Practising Midwife, MIDIRS Midwifery Digest and The British Journal of Midwifery, which all came on the scene after

Midwifery Matters, there is still a real need for a magazine that can publish articles that others would reject as being too political, fringe or way-out. In this increasingly secular society, I also feel that there needs to be a forum which can acknowledge the spiritual aspects of midwifery. Sometimes the technological and clinical aspects of birth seem to overshadow everything else. Is there a radical midwife who has not read Ina May Gaskin 's Spiritual Midwifery - even if they don't agree with every word? Where else can similar material be published in the UK if not within ARM 's magazine? And if it goes over the top occasionally then at least it gets people talking and debating about what is and what is not relevant to midwifery in the twenty-first century. The Letters page seems to have been a bit thin on the ground recently compared to earlier days of ARM. Please write in and join the debates. It is your magazine.

Margaret Jowitt
Midwifery Matters 93 – Summer 2002

Midwife Voice

D - student midwife - '*...I think I have a slight aversion to the word radical, despite being quite involved in the Association of Radical Midwives. Both because each time I bring up the ARM with a friend or contact of mine, I have to preface it with, 'it doesn't mean radical like trans exclusionary radical feminist.' That's not the meaning of radical in this context and so because of that connotation, it can be quite difficult and I think also because I think the type of midwifery that the ARM promotes, and uplifts, and focuses on, and teaches is not, or shouldn't be considered that radical; It's normal, appropriate, midwifery care and so it's exciting to be "like we're radical". But also, it shouldn't be considered something scary and non-mainstream to focus on consent and choice and good quality care...*'

Midwife Voice

K - community midwife and long-time ARM member - '*...from* *the beginning that's how it's been for me; that's why probably, I became a midwife. I was really fortunate that I started [in] 1992 and our course co-ordinator was just very, very normal based, and that was fundamental to how our training was. I was lucky I suppose. I've been lucky in many ways, but I've tended to have midwives that were quite... again that normality. I think it's just always keeping that in mind, and always keeping women in mind. I've gone through phases, probably in the last few years, where you think, I don't know, suppose being part of the system, sometimes it's really difficult. But it's still... it's just, just keeping true to being there for women all the time. I suppose I've been lucky that I just managed to get, I know it sounds terrible here, but almost feel that you've got away with it in a lot of ways. You actually can give women that support and care, and yeah, just them being at the centre of everything. Sometimes I think I'm just, you know, I mean I've worked on the community for the last 20-22 years. [It] probably does give you a bit more freedom. I know I could never go back to being in that sort of labour ward type thing, but yeah... it's just things that to me is... ARM. I think we had somebody that told us about [ARM] that first term in University, and that's when I joined...'*

Birth of a midwife

I came to midwifery as a profession comparatively late; I had given birth three times and was 31 years old. Those three years training full-time, with children aged 10, 7 and 5 years old when I began, were the hardest of my life (Walcott 1997). Engaging in studying again fifteen years after leaving school, having to work shifts in hospital and community, along with caring for my family, it was only my absolute passion for birth, to be *with woman*, that held me in those years... that, and the Association of Radical Midwives (ARM).

I discovered ARM in 1989, five years before I eventually became a student midwife. My passion for midwifery had begun with my first experience of birth to my daughter in 1983 - this was when my education as a midwife really started. I began reading about birth, midwifery and anything associated with it. After each subsequent birth experience, my resolve to one day be a midwife grew. My first son was born in 1987 and by that time I was deeply involved with La Leche League (LLL) an organisation that supports breastfeeding mothers. It was at one of their conferences in 1989, just after I'd had my second son (at home) that I heard a midwife from ARM speak. Immediately I joined ARM as an associate member and began planning my future as a professional midwife.

In the five years running up to applying to train as a midwife, I attended as many ARM national meetings as possible, even when living overseas in Belgium for three years (my first husband was in the RAF). I worked as an American Red Cross Volunteer for three years in an American Army Field Hospital whilst in Belgium (Walcott 1993). Two or three mornings a week, I was part of the staff team in the Obstetric Clinic, chaperoning, administrating, essentially the job that an antenatal clinic maternity assistant would do in the UK. I even trained to give the antenatal classes, along with home studies to gain more GCSEs in readiness for applying for midwifery education. I ensured that family visits home to the UK coincided with ARM meet-ups. I'd found my tribe, my people, a sisterhood of women who shared a philosophy of birth that felt entirely right to me but was at odds with the direction the profession had seemed to have taken since the 1970s.

The following is the text of the very first article that I had published in Midwifery Matters. It was written just before I began my midwifery training.

Article

Birth in an American army 'field' hospital (Belgium)

I have been an Associate Member of ARM for two years, and wrote about my desire to become a midwife in Issue 48 of *Mid-*

wifery Matters 1991. I am currently living in Belgium, but this year expect to return to the UK and consequently will be able to apply for a preregistration midwifery course. I've spent the last couple of years obtaining the necessary GCSEs, and gaining invaluable work experience as a volunteer for the American Red Cross.

I was expecting things to be different to the antenatal care I'd experienced as a British mother in an NHS hospital, but what surprised me more was how much real 'nursing midwifery' I was allowed to do as a non-medical volunteer.

On an OB (obstetric) morning, I screen the clients before they see the obstetrician. Testing urine, weighing them and taking their blood pressure. I then act as a chaperone, and there is always endless paperwork as well as cleaning and stocking exam rooms.

Gyn (gynaecology) mornings are sometimes even more interesting as I not only screen the patients, I am allowed to assist the doctors in many minor procedures which are performed in the clinic; smear tests, colposcopy, IUD insertions and removals and even endometrial and cervical biopsies.

I now have additional responsibilities having qualified as a Red Cross instructor teaching the 'Healthy Pregnancy, Healthy Baby' course. Basically it is the same as antenatal classes, although this course seems far more detailed than I remember classes in Britain to be, except that here the emphasis is on medical knowledge rather than the emotional side of things. To qualify as a candidate to instruct I had to answer a hundred question test and obtain over 80%. I was terrified at the time as I was taking the course with some obstetric nurses. I need not have worried as I actually scored 93%.

We have a huge cross-section of expectant mums here: 15 nationalities, including American, British, other Europeans, and even some mums from the Middle East. So the attitudes and traditions with which we have to be aware are very wide-ranging, although in practice few alternatives may be offered, for instance, there are no female obstetricians available.

A large proportion of our mums are American Service on active duty. They work up until the birth and then have six weeks before returning to duty. At three months post-partum they have a physical trainman test, where they are also expected to be back to their pre-pregnancy weight. If they are not, they are referred to the dietician for six months. And then if they are still overweight, they are discharged from the service.

There are some excellent advantages from being under the American system of care here, as they are very much into preventative medicine; smear tests are done on all adult women annually, mammograms are first done at age 35 for a future reference, and every two years from the of age 40, depending on the results, then a woman may even have mammograms every year. Money is clearly no object here. What this means for the expectant mothers is that every test imaginable is available. This of course can be both a disadvantage and an advantage, as tests such as the unpleasant test for diabetes which involves starving the expectant mother for up to 12 hours, are automatically performed on all mums at 28 weeks. On the plus side, tests such as the AFP blood test are offered to all. But nobody is ever allowed to deliver here unless they also agree to an HIV test.

British mothers find the constant tests somewhat unnecessary in general, but some are reassured, and American mums positively expect everything.

There is of course also a higher caesarean rate (higher than UK, but lower than the USA) around 22%. American mothers find this encouraging but British mothers are more concerned. There are no VBACs, a breech is always a caesarean, but they do sometimes attempt to turn the baby. No mother ever seems to labour for much more than a day (unless she has strong objections to interventions).

But the greatest advantage I have experienced form working here is that I am able to see births. I have been present at four births so far; two caesareans and two vaginal deliveries, and acting as a birth coach for one mother staying with her for eight hours while she was in labour.

Mothers are encouraged to spend the early hours of labour at home unless their membranes rupture. Once here, they have a standard half hour or so on the monitor. VEs (or pelvic exams as they call them here) are infrequent until the mother nears the end of the first stage but then may be every contraction. ARM appears standard at 6cm dilation. There are no restrictions on movement, or position during the first stage, a shower is available, and the only analgesic is Demerol, but they also use a pudendal block which at first I could not see the point of as mothers did not seem to gain any relief, then I read in an American obstetric book that a pudendal block allows an episiotomy to be performed. Episiotomy is common here especially on first deliveries as they do not like mothers to be long in the second stage, but the third stage is achieved without drugs unless there are complications. Fathers are encouraged to cut the cord, but then the baby is taken away for a standard observation on various monitors for the first hour or two although if the mother is aware of this practice she may discuss this in advance with the paediatrician and arrange for the monitoring to be done later. Few mothers either know or are concerned, although when I was teaching the antenatal classes I stressed the importance of bonding in the early hours and particularly encouraged mothers choosing to breastfeed to attempt to do so in the first hour.

Dissolving stitches are used, and witch hazel pads can be purchased to soothe as well as a sitz bath (a sort of mini bidet). Bathing is advised against until after the postpartum check.

Rooming-in is standard and breastfeeding is encouraged unless the baby is jaundiced. A pump is available, but the slightest rise in bilirubin is seen as potentially harmful and many mothers become discouraged. My attempts to change this policy failed.

In general I do not think that the care here is any worse than in a British hospital, in fact there are some advantages; here you get to see the person who is going to deliver your baby at every visit to the clinic. But having had a baby at home nothing else can compare. Although practices here are different, I do find that

Americans are extremely friendly and cheerful. We 'Brits' can be too serious about things.

All in all I am extremely grateful to the Americans to have had an opportunity to gain such experience.

Lynn Walcott
Midwifery Matters 57 – Summer 1993

Midwife Voice
M - student midwife (similar history to me) - *'...I think for me, being radical means going back to the reason I started this in the first place, which was wanting to help women have normal births. I was a La Leche League leader, and I would see breastfeeding problems, and I'd think... if only they hadn't had such problems at birth, maybe things would be easier, so now I'm going to be a midwife. I'm feeling positive and I know some things, some people are going to be high risk, and then you're going to have to help them by intervening, but I think a lot of the time, we don't need to. But going back, going back to why I wanted to do it, going back to how people can actually give birth, I think it fits with what I want to do, and who I am. I radically un-school my children. I didn't realise they'd even had the same word, of radical in there. I explained to my husband, that's what it actually means. He's like, I didn't know that, but it's just something that we do - we feel happy with. Actually, I've come back to realising now, I want to get back to why I wanted to do this in the first place ...'*

Midwife Voice
Q - a student's journey to being a midwife - *'being radical, I think I was born into this position. I am this place in the biosphere almost. [laughs]. You know, I used to say I was my mum's little nurse. She passed away when I was five. She was in her third trimester and then she had a brain haemorrhage, and the doctors didn't believe her - that she was having these headaches - and had a, you know, a tough time. After that, I genuinely think that had they believed her, I would have become a midwife earlier. But everywhere I went, even though I had a different career, I was finding that I was staying with midwives. So you know, it's almost like it's a perennial presence in my*

DNA, like I was gathering nourishment, like I gravitated towards ARM. I found myself staying with two sisters, two Mayan midwives. Didn't even know that they were midwives until about the second day, you know, and you do find yourself sort of gathering in, listening, learning, and I didn't even know that's what I was doing, you know? Yeah, there's a few instances like that, in various travels. But yeah, I would say, that I supported a few births, just a handful, and in between, then, to having my own, and then changed career and I found myself thinking, hold on a minute, that birth is not how it's meant to be, with my first. Being able to support... to support the woman yes, but I love reading research, I really, really do. But it's that sort of dusk, of listening, let it percolate. Okay, what's true right now for you, what's important, and then going with that. So I supported. I couldn't call myself a midwife and I wasn't doing anything clinical...so, I've started training and it's been hard. It's been really hard. I feel a bit like it's mortifying the body and the mind in order to one day, be in a position where I might find myself... where I can actually make more influence above the ground, and then come back down again, and then pop up somewhere else. [laughs]. Although I recognise that my vocation has never come from a PIN [personal identification number given to registered midwives in the UK]. *We are working with social constructs, but I think everything looks the same, and being with the ARM, I feel nourished... As a 41 year old woman, who you know, I'm not a wimp [laugh], it's hard, it's absolutely hard and having you all there, yeah, it actually really makes a big difference. To get to the end of this week, I knew I was going to be tired, but I wanted to stay awake because it nourishes me - to just sit with you. So, thank you.'*

Coven contribution - My life with ARM

1980 At the age of 51, after 28 years of family life in Iran with my Iranian husband, bringing up 2 girls and a boy, we returned to England. My asthma was part of the reason, and Reza had taken early retirement from the Oil Company. The situation in

Iran, Radical Islamic Rule, had forced the change.

We had already bought a house in Ormskirk. As Reza's pension was not paid outside Iran, he tried many times to get a decent job, but could only find work as a night watchman, so I had to become the breadwinner.

With SRN and Part 1 Midwifery qualifications, I applied to the local hospital for work. I was offered a place as Staff Nurse on one of the surgical wards, but I turned it down, as my practical experience was nearly 30 years ago. I went to the Maternity Unit, for a job as an auxiliary, (at least I could do the bedpan rounds and bath babies!). The Senior Midwife, seeing my qualifications told me there was vacancy for a staff-nurse in the antenatal clinic, helping the midwives. I accepted the offer, provided I could wear a white coat instead of the staff-nurse uniform, to avoid being called to an emergency! She agreed to this, and suggested that I join the student nurses studying the Maternity Care Module, to bring myself up to date, which was very helpful. I enjoyed the work, among very friendly and supportive fellow midwives.

One day Miss Ross Jones came up to speak to me. "I think you should complete your midwifery training. It's only a one year course for State Registered Nurses, like you. Please think about it". I was flattered that she thought I was capable, but I wasn't keen, a whole year of studying while working full-time? A couple of weeks later she asked me if I had applied for the course, and I told her about my concerns. She wasn't convinced. To show her it wasn't such a good idea, I wrote to the CMB asking about the criteria for post SRN training, giving my age, which I thought would bring a "Sorry, too old" reply. It didn't; the response was 'find a training course'!

September 1981 found me in Fazakerly Maternity Hospital, Liverpool, as one of a group of students. Most of them had just completed SRN, and were mostly in their early twenties. A woman in her thirties, having worked as a Staff Nurse, was also joining the course. As an "oldie" I was made very welcome, and we became a very supportive group. There were four tutors running the course, and we all agreed that with Wendy Barnes, we had the best of the bunch. She had a very open style, inviting comments throughout, which stimulated some lively exchanges. She was very patient with us, especially with me. I couldn't resist commenting on the vast difference between current midwifery practice and that which I'd experienced in London, 30 years earlier.

Things had changed so much since 1951. The system of care was now so medicalised; dating scans early in pregnancy setting the "due" date; women being admitted on that date, (to have their labour started by rupture of membranes); being continuously monitored by a sensor strapped around the abdomen, and when considered ready to give birth, being transferred to the labour rooms for the actual birth.

After a couple of months I'd begun to despair of becoming what I called a 'real' midwife, and was seriously thinking about giving up the course. I then read about a group calling itself AIMS, (Association for improvements in Maternity Services), and joined them. The letter from Beverly Beech suggested that I also contact another organisation, recently set up, of midwives trying to bring more normality to childbirth care, calling themselves the Association of Radical Midwives. ('Radical' taken from the dictionary, meaning "roots and origins"; i.e. of true midwifery). This sounded promising and I was invited to visit the local branch in Lancashire.

Dressed "smartly", I knocked on the door, which was opened by a woman dressed as I could only describe as 'Hippy'. It was an eye opener to find myself sipping coffee with half a dozen young women similarly garbed, discussing the finer points of woman-centred midwifery care. I was hooked! Explaining my situation, and my disappointment with the heavily interventionist system of the training course, they persuaded me to complete it and become my own kind of Midwife. I took their advice, qualified as a midwife, started work in Ormskirk Maternity Unit, where there was somewhat less interference with the natural processes of childbirth.

ARM was foremost in my working life ever since that day, and after retirement I was able to give more time to the day-to-day work, membership was growing, and ARM itself became well-organised, registered as a genuine Charitable Organisation with a fee to be paid, in return for support. We started a quarterly Newsletter, typed and copied, posted out to members, which eventually grew to become the quarterly Magazine, with the title, Midwifery Matters, chosen by members' votes at a well-attended quarterly meeting.

I was just going to say I feel that radical was normal for me at one time.

Ishbel Kargar

Article

Let Midwives be Born Again

"The Midwives Were Fantastic!"

How often do we hear those words? Actually, probably fairly regularly. Our midwives are fantastic... aren't they?

I was in the changing rooms at the local swimming pool recently and, as usual, there were the mothers with their toddlers after swimming class. Two women next to me, one pregnant, were having a conversation about the impending birth. My ears always prick with excitement listening to such conversations – once a midwife, always a midwife – but these days, I keep my own counsel.

Near to her due date, expecting her third child, the main concern was whether or not she would get to the hospital in time; her husband was an hour and a half away at work, both sets of grandparents were over two hours away, and most friends, although happy to help if possible, had regular commitments. She planned to hop in a taxi and just inform the school as the last time she'd only just made it to the hospital, and as her first was a LSCS (lower segment caesarean section) she was deemed too high risk for a homebirth! Well, I could write this entire article about my thought process at the time of 'the ridiculousness of the assessment of risk in this case for a home birth?' But I won't... something else piqued my interest.

The other woman was reflecting on her own births; "The midwives were fantastic!" She seemed to repeat this in various forms over and over again – she just couldn't 'thank them enough', she was 'forever grateful' and 'they were so amazing'... the adjectives were reeled off. Initially I was feeling rather smug about my profession and so pleased that the hard-pressed NHS local midwifery staff were being praised, at a hospital that most women seemed to have little good to say.

But then I realised what else she was saying, that they had both been LSCSs, she had been so high risk, and when it 'all started to go wrong', how wonderful and professional everyone was. Great? I'm not so sure?

It dawned on me what I hear so often. Yes – the midwives are fantastic... when there's an emergency LSCS going on.

However, as I said, the norm when talking about the local service was dire – women left alone, women not supported, women frightened, the list of complaints I have heard in this very changing room over the last couple of years is astounding... and one thing in common... these were the 'normal' births – the low risk, trouble free vaginal births.

What does this say about the service the midwives at my local hospital offer? A straw poll of sorts I admit, but in all honesty, I cannot remember a single 'fantastic midwife' at any of the so called normal birth stories recounted here. But, this 'fantastic midwives' story at a LSCS was not the first... actually, it may possibly be every LSCS has these elusive 'fantastic midwives' present.

What can I deduce from these reflections? Is it the women's perspectives only? Do they feel 'saved', grateful that the unsupported frightening labour has been curtailed by such efficiency......with a smile? Is it simply that the service, pushed to the limit is managed well, working on principles of prioritisation, those in most need getting the best of it? Or is it, as I suspect, that the midwives are in fact 'medwives', more comfortable in their roles administering medical rather than midwifery care? This is safe, supported, and fits into the system's ethos, essentially it is less stressful to work in this way. Is it, as with my own experience in the NHS, that we are trained to deliver good medical care, but must learn to be real midwives once on the job, and that is near impossible to do in a service stretched to breaking point?

Whatever the truth of it, it is my experience and it is my opinion, and it makes me sad.

I spent years preparing to become a midwife; studying GCSEs at home with three young children, doing volunteer work, absorbing all I could in the world of birth. I subscribed to the NCT, ARM, AIMS, MIDIRS and other journals, read book after book, always my favourite; *Spiritual Midwifery* by Ina May Gaskin. I had four child-minders in the three years as a student midwife, travelled thousands of miles, working shifts, doing a university course – it was exhausting and exhilarating. And then I qualified, got my first job, and realised that I knew nothing... well, very little about being a midwife, but loads about how to work as a midwife in the NHS.

Hospital, then community and within two years independent practice – eventually I was the midwife I wanted to be. I know that I made an impression on women's lives, as they did on my life. It has been almost the most satisfying and absorbing thing I have ever done, second only to motherhood itself!

I do hope that for the sake of my granddaughters, and all future mothers that we get back to our roots and be Radical...

Are doulas now the real midwives?

This is a strong and controversial statement I realise, and in truth, I don't believe it simply as it stands, but I do believe there is a potential here that I'd like to explore.

'Midwife' – 'with woman', we all know the meaning and take pride in it as midwives. 'Doula' – a woman who assists in childbirth, this is a dictionary meaning. A dictionary meaning of midwife is 'somebody who is trained to deliver babies'. Looking from this perspective, I actually see that I have mostly been a doula, I assist – 'pizzas are delivered, babies are born'!

Lynn Genevieve
Midwifery Matters 137 – Summer 2013

Midwife Voice

J – an ARM member who was first a doula, then a midwife - *'I was a doula - I didn't even know it. When I was 18, a friend of mine who was 19, had a termination due to abnormality incompatible with life, and I went to the hospital with her. And when after the baby was born, she said "I want to see it" and the midwife said, (I didn't even know midwifery was a thing) the midwife said "oh, no you don't, it's just a mass of blood and clots, you don't want to see it," and my friend kinda shrank. And I said, "she does - I do - we do - we want to meet this person." And she came in with it, in a you know, metal kidney dish with green towel on the top, and just went "ugh!" We sat and we held her baby, and we named her, and we cried. And I held her, and I didn't know that I was 'doula-ing' until 20 years later, when I kind of formalised that. So for me, it's like radically supporting people in that liminal time, in our culture, where there is lots of fear and misinformation. I became a midwife, because I wanted more knowledge to better support. I didn't really want to be a midwife, [laughs] I did the training because I needed to... to learn more, so that I could better support people. And then I thought I'd just leave it up to the universe, and the universe has got me where I am now.*

What does it mean to me to be radical? To utterly have at the core of my practise, that... the person birthing, and those around them, know what's right for them, and they know they need somebody to guide, support, signpost, show them that they're worth the care, that they are worth being served by us, and then they make the right decisions for them. It's their body - their baby - their life. I cannot have any judgement; I have no right. All my job is to support them, to achieve what they want...'

The Birth of ARM

Here is the text of an article that appeared in Issue 1 of the ARM Newsletter that became Midwifery Matters June 1978.

Article

Labour Pains - How the Association of Radical Midwives was Born

In the early spring of 1976 another student and I met as she was just starting to do midwifery training in a Northern hospital and I was halfway through mine in the Midlands. For the next three days we shared books, newsletters, information, and most importantly, support. We were afraid that in the present surge of obstetric interference we would never learn how to be true midwives: women who are 'with women' in pregnancy and childbirth, and who are caretakers of normal birth, women who use their hands, eyes, and ears as sensitive, diagnostic tools, who are patient, knowledgeable and supportive.

We concluded that if there were two of us who were so dissatisfied there must be more.

The word spread by mouth, and in the early summer of 1976 we held our first meeting in London with ten student midwives and one staff midwife. We talked about what we had observed in hospitals around the country, discovering that what was considered vital to the safety of the mother and baby in one hospital wasn't considered so in another. We resolved to determine the difference between the expedient and the necessary in obstetrics. The Association of Radical Midwives (then without a name) was born. Since the London meeting two years ago there have been 15 meetings on a national level, and regional groups have started to hold their own meetings. We now have about 20 people at our six-weekly weekend meetings, with more than 150 people on our current mailing list.

It took us about a year to name ourselves. By that time we were becoming more outspoken about the political implications of the present and projected future role of the midwife. We had an article in the *Sunday Times* in July 1977 which started communication with about 100 midwives, most feeling as angry and isolated as we. We also had small articles printed in *Baby Newsline*, a Johnson and Johnson publication *Spare Rib, Peace News* and a bit in *Our Bodies Ourselves Women's Health Packet.*

Since the beginning of the group, changes have started to take place in obstetrics. Studies, such as Ian Chalmers' Cardiff survey, have given the obstetricians reasons to curtail wholesale induction. Some women are demanding a more sensitive approach to obstetrics. On the other hand, domiciliary midwives are losing ground fast, and post-natal nurses are being hired to replace midwives. The Department of Health and Social Security is cutting back more than £10 million in maternity services in the next 5 years, and home deliveries are almost extinct. It's a continuing struggle.

Like any group, we have had growing pains concerning structure, ideology and policy. By the Wycombe meeting in September 1977 we had found the need to organise ourselves in a more structured way (see Jenny Spink's article) and at present we are trying to learn more and more about the overall situation of midwifery in this country, as well as forming links with other midwifery groups both here and abroad.

Marianne Scruggs

Bringing us up to date, this is the 'about us' page, of ARM's website https://www.midwifery.org.uk/about-us/ setting out who they are and what they believe today.

Welcome to the ARM

We are midwives, student midwives and others committed to improving maternity services in the UK and internationally. We strongly believe that all women have the right to a service tailored closely to their needs, and a sympathetic attitude on the part of their professional attendants.

The Association of Radical Midwives provides support and information for those wishing to give or receive good sympathetic, personalised midwifery care. We are stakeholders in policy-making at local, national and international level and we're involved with many campaigns and projects relating to midwifery and maternity care. We have contacts and local groups all around UK, as well as our overseas members.

We are a UK Registered Charity, No.1060525

Our Vision

is for autonomous, empowered midwives to be able to support women's choices in childbirth. We believe that midwifery matters. The full version of our vision is available here.

Our Mission

is to provide support, information, leadership and practical assistance for midwives, student midwives and others so that maternity services are woman-centred, compassionate and human-scaled.

What are our objectives?

- To re-establish the confidence of the midwife in her own skills as an autonomous practitioner
- To share ideals, skills and information
- To provide support and care for midwives, other health professionals and maternity service users
- To provide leadership in campaigns to further our vision

- To encourage midwives in their support of women's active participation in birth
- To reaffirm the need for midwives to provide continuity of carer
- To explore and support midwives in delivering alternative patterns of care
- To encourage evaluation of developments in our field

How did we start?

The Association of Radical Midwives (ARM) was formed in 1976 by a small group of student midwives from different training schools who were alarmed by the apparent trend towards maternity nurse status in their training. The acronym 'ARM' is a pun on the term 'Artificial Rupture of Membranes' which was routinely (over-) used at the time. Read our full history here.

Why "Radical"?

The word 'Radical' is used in its literary meaning of relating to roots and origins, and best expresses the hope of that early group, that midwifery could find its way back to a position where midwives' skills were used to the full, while still taking advantage of the benefits of modern technological advances, where these are seen to be in the best interests of the woman and her child. In other words, the hope that the true meaning of midwife ('with woman') will once more be realised in practice.

Coven contributor

I joined the Association of Radical Midwives in 1976, I went to the International Confederation of Midwives in Glasgow with Mary Cronk and we stayed at her Mum's house. At the time the name for the Organisation hadn't been fixed but it had to be ARM because that was the most frequent intervention in childbirth at the time and was written on every woman's line on the whiteboard in the Labour Ward. So would it be the Association of Randy Midwives, or Research Based Midwives or Real Midwives? Radical was decided upon because we were very radical at the time but when this caused great offence to EVERYONE we backtracked and said that it was radical as in roots.

We used to meet monthly, all bringing sleeping bags and sleeping in someone's house. Every month we wept and wept over the state of midwifery in the UK. Finally Marianne Scruggs said that if we did nothing but weep we'd never achieve anything, so it was decided that we would write the Vision - our Vision of how we wanted midwifery to be in the UK.

We held the meeting at my house because I had a computer and printer (Unusual in those days) and in order to come to this meeting people had to write a two page draft of their ideas. You couldn't just rock up on the day without having put some work in first. My husband Giles went to stay with my Mother and my children went to friends. I cooked tons of veggie stews mainly made up of beans.

The Organisation was founded by Marianne Scruggs - a genius from the USA, Judy Rogers from Canada and Lidwin Jury from Australia. With Marianne's foresight we produced "The Vision" from all our ideas. I typed whilst people called out what they wanted in it.

We got the publication bound and printed, Gilly Rosser's Mum gave us £1,000 to get it publicised and we sent it to every MP, every midwife leader, the RCOG - you name it, they got a copy.

If you notice, every subsequent Maternity Document has been based on the Vision - Changing Childbirth, Better Births etc etc I feel very proud to have been part of it.

I am also very, very impressed by Midwives Haven which has saved the sanity of many midwives up before the NMC which is a cruel and unjust Organisation.

What do we need to do next? I think we have to get PII for Independent Midwives - they lead the profession and whilst they are so emasculated they have no voice and the independence of the profession is at huge risk.

The RCM is not really there for midwives or women. I remember when the Vision came out, I was on the Council and the jeering and mickey taking had to be heard to be believed. The NMC hates midwives and tried to destroy them - because strong midwives are such a nuisance and won't do what they are told!!

Caroline Flint RN RM ADM

Midwife Voice

N – long-time ARM member - '...*I went somewhere else in a different hospital, and in 1980, the Short Report came out, and everything changed...and medicalised, and I started to be medicalized as well. And I was quite proud of it; I was quite proud of working out very efficiently on a labour ward. You know, doing everything right - time limits and everything. Although one thing, good thing was that we were very, very encouraged not to use episiotomies, so that was fine. But I suddenly started to realise what's going on, and fortunately, I found the ARM...*'

FEMINISM

Coven contributor

Radical to me meant being different and offering something different through other ways of caring for women during the continuum of pregnancy, birth and motherhood.

I initially stood back from ARM, even though those I knew to be members, were the midwives I most admired and I valued their ways of thinking and doing.

However, ARM was about women's voices and as a man who happened to be a midwife, my voice was not what they wanted to hear, but my ways of working supported continuity of care and encouraged the centrality and focus of the needs of the mother and her family.

Eventually, I was encouraged to join ARM. As a member, I fully subscribed to the movements values and active motivation to improve and advance maternity care. These radical midwives worked hard to enhance and encourage new ways of working. They made a difference to the profession of midwifery as well as our obstetric colleagues. Importantly, they made a positive difference in the lives of the women they served.

Part 2
Paul Lewis

Article

A.R.M. in a changing world (1976 – 2016) Irene Walton

This year is the 40th anniversary of A.R.M. and I have been reflecting on some of the changes that have taken place during its lifetime. Co-incidentally it came into being the year I became a midwife.

The 1970's were a period of great societal as well as midwifery change. In 1976 female contraception was relatively new; the 1960s had given women the pill (with its high dosages and problems) the swinging sixties and the beginnings of changing sexual attitudes. However, women were still second class citizens in many ways and had fewer rights than men. In the U.K. the Equal Pay Act (1970) had only come into force in December 1975. The 'baby boomers' following World War II were now adults and wanted more of everything especially choice. In 1968 there had been a resurgence of interest in Simone de Beauvoir's 1949 book "The Second Sex" which led to the second wave feminist movement and the formation of Le Mouvement de Libération des Femmes (The Women's Liberation Movement). There were writers such as Betty Friedan (1963), Germaine Greer (1970) and Dale Spender (1980) whose influence had led to a wider discussion of women's' issues, sexist terminology and legal inequalities in areas such as domestic violence, rape and reproductive rights. Women were beginning to be less passive and become more assertive (Harne 2010). Until now they had been trained from birth by the example of parents, family structure, society and the media to aspire to marriage and motherhood as the ideal. Now a movement was afoot that identified and named the problems that women faced and wanted to abolish sexism. This was the period that saw the establishment of women's refuges, rape crisis centres, and changes in divorce and custody laws and reproductive rights. These rights were first discussed at the United Nation's 1968 International Conference on Human

Rights. They included the right to contraception, legal and safe abortion, sexual health education, reproductive choices and freedom from female genital mutilation, forced contraception and sterilization.

From 1948 until 1974 midwives were employed in a tripartite system where maternity care was divided between hospitals, general practitioners and the local authorities. Midwives were normally employed as district midwives by the local authority or worked in and were employed by the hospital. Women had their babies at home, in a maternity home or in hospital. Hospital beds were in short supply and unless there were complications the first baby was born at home or in a maternity home and subsequent children were born at home. There was little choice in the matter.

Then as now the NHS was costing the Government money and earlier the Guillebaud (1956) inquiry (set up to review the cost) had found the system to be in "confusion" and recommended further investigation. This was carried out by the Earl of Cranbrook who published the 1959 Report of the Maternity Services Committee (the Cranbrook report) which recommended that with proper selection 70% of women should give birth in hospital and 30% would be fine to give birth at home. This was rapidly taken on board and obstetricians continued to push for more hospitalization of women and the concept of risk was formulated. In 1967 a further review of the maternity services was carried out by the Maternity and Midwifery Advisory Committee chaired by Sir John Peel. The Peel Report (Ministry of Health 1970) was published in 1970 and suggested that hospital birth was safest and that all women should give birth in hospital cared for by a team of doctors, midwives and general practitioners. It recommended that small isolated obstetric units should be phased out and be replaced by consultant/general practitioner units in general hospitals and that there should be a 100% hospital confinement rate. Very little evidence was put forward in support of this view and certainly no account was taken of women's views on the matter.

From 1970 there was a huge change in the service with women being sent to hospital to give birth, and a change in the structure of the maternity service with all NHS midwives being employed in an integrated service based on the hospital. Following the Peel Report the home birth rate has remained at approximately 5%. Not only were women having to give birth in hospital they were being subjected more and more to interventions and procedures such as episiotomy (Before 1967 this was not even in the sphere of practice of a midwife), inductions involving artificial rupture of the membranes and oxytocic drips, soap enemas (high, hot and helluva lot), increased vaginal examinations and caesarean sections.

It was into this climate that The Association of Radical Midwives (A.R.M.) was born. I was a student midwife in the same hospital when one of the founders was also a student midwife there. It is generally thought that ARM was brought about as a reaction to the routine procedures such as episiotomies but in reality it was much more than that. It was (and still is) a truly autonomous, egalitarian, woman centred, feminist organisation with no hierarchy.

The 1980's opened with the publication of the `Short report' as the second report from the Social Services Committee (House of Commons 1979-80) on Perinatal and Neonatal Mortality chaired by Renee Short was commonly known. Midwives, ARM and RCM members and pressure groups such as AIMs and the NCT were all hoping for some light in the darkness of the maternity services but this was not to be. It agreed unequivocally with the Peel Report that there should be a 100% hospital confinement and additionally recommended that home deliveries be further phased out. Although looking at ways to prevent morbidity and mortality the Short Report not only supported the status quo but said that labour wards should be staffed and equipped as intensive care wards and recommended an increase in the number of obstetricians and gynaecologists. It also recommended that continuous recording of the fetal heart rate should increasingly become part of the surveillance of all babies during labour.

Little was discussed about the woman at the receiving end of all this technical and impersonal care or the midwives who were trying to give individual and supportive care to women whilst working in a system of increasing restrictions and rules. However it did recognise that the skills of the midwife should be made better use of and also that continuity of care for the woman was an ideal to be aspired to. It stated that;

Midwifery is the cornerstone of British obstetric practice yet it is our impression from the evidence we have taken that never in this century, has morale amongst midwives been at such a low ebb.

and

We recommend that every effort is made to re-establish midwifery as a profession that offers attractive prospects to young women interested in a nursing career.

(House of Commons 1979-80. Short Report. page 76)

It also identified a need for the maternity services to become more humanised because it did not consider it enough to concentrate solely on the physical wellbeing of the mother and her baby.

The emotional support provided by the maternity services, although more difficult to define, is also of major importance.

(House of Commons 1979-80 Short Report. page 91).

Following the Short report the Government set up the Maternity Advisory Committee which produced three reports which were to be very influential in the planning of maternity care in the 1980s. They were Maternity Care in Action Part 1 - Antenatal care, Part 2 - Care during Childbirth and Part 3 - Care of the Mother and Baby (1982, 1984, 1985). These little booklets were used as guidelines by Maternity Service Liaison committees, Heads of Midwifery Service, obstetricians and Health Authorities in order to provide a good standard of maternity care. They also maintained that the best place to have one's baby was in the maternity unit and so hospital confinement was again reinforced as being the safest and best type of care. This was not agreed by everyone and one of the most eminent dissenters in the field was Marjorie Tew (1990) who highlighted the fact that statistically a causal relationship could not be found between the fall in the perinatal mortality figures and hospital confinement. She says:

> *The correlation which obstetricians and others claim between increasing medical care, or specific obstetric interventions, and decreasing mortality are quickly shown to be spurious. They all fall at the first hurdle, so that further analysis is never necessary.*
>
> *(Tew, M 1990 page 268)*

ARM members started to rally and work with the women's groups to support women in the right to have a gentle, supported birth at home or in hospital. They met in each other's homes and in 1978 began to produce a newsletter which has now become this magazine Midwifery Matters. A.R.M. was in many ways the organisation that highlighted the frustration felt by many midwives and mothers with the segmented pattern of care and the need for midwives to be practitioners in their own right. In 1986 the A.R.M. published its proposals for the future of the maternity services in a document entitled `The Vision' (A.R.M. 1986). The Vision which had been devised by a working party of midwives set out basic principles which were eventually taken on board by the Winterton report. These were:

> 1. *That the relationship between mother and midwife is fundamental to good midwifery care (p 20).*
> 2. *That the mother is the central person in the process of care (p 21).*
> 3. *Informed choice in childbirth for women (p 22).*
> 4. *Full utilization of midwives' skills (pp 23, 24).*
> 5. *Continuity of care for all childbearing women (pp 24a, 25, 26).*
> 6. *Community based care (pp 6,15a, 20)*
> 7. *Accountability of services to those receiving them (p 4).*
> 8. *Care should do no harm to mother and baby (p 2).*
>
> (The Vision (1986)

The Health Committee of the House of Commons chaired by Nicholas Winterton, MP carried out an investigation into the maternity services in 1991/2. Evidence was taken from 446 memoranda from individuals or organisations which included the A.R.M, midwives, obstetricians and women themselves. The report looked at policy developments in the maternity services, what women actually want, the evidence from the professionals, the regional services, the maternity services of the future, and the way forward. It concluded that encouraging all women to give birth in hospital could not be justified on the grounds of safety and that the pattern of maternity should not be driven on a medical model of care based on unproven assertions. It considered that women needed to have informed choice with women being given;

> *...sufficient, balanced non-judgemental and appropriate information at each stage of the maternity process.*
> (House of Commons Winterton Report 1992-2 page xvii)

When taking evidence from the three Royal colleges, the Royal College of Midwives (RCM), the Royal College of Obstetricians and Gynaecologists (RCOG) and the Royal College of General Practitioners (RCGP) the Committee felt that they seemed to be more concerned with which group should have control over the maternity services and their rivalries loomed large. The Association of Radical Midwives (ARM) identified the medical model of care as being the main impediment to the delivery of team midwifery and a `midwifery led' service.

The Committee was not convinced that the organisation of the maternity services had succeeded in resolving the conflicts between the various philosophies of care. It went on to look at various aspects of care and made several recommendations aimed at improving practice and developing research based practice. It also recommended that small units should not be closed on the grounds of safety and that they should remain as an option for women. Team midwifery and case loading were recommended as a way of providing continuity of care for women and as a best practice model. Overall it said,

> *That the woman having a baby should be seen as the focus of care; and that the professionals providing that care should identify their needs and develop arrangements to meet them which are based on full and equal co-operation between all those charged with her care.*
> (House of Commons Winterton Report 1991-2)

In addition the report looked at the education, research, evaluation and audit issues surrounding good practice in the maternity services and concluded, interestingly, amongst other things that midwifery should be afforded the same rights as other professions over the control of its education, and there should be a midwifery research funding body set up to enable the expansion of research by midwives. The Winterton Report found much to criticise about the maternity services but it acknowledged in particular the skill of the midwife, the obstetrician and the paediatrician. As a result of this report an Expert Maternity Group chaired by Baroness Cumberlege was set up to report in detail on the way forward for the Maternity Service and its report entitled Changing Childbirth (Department of Health 1993) was published at the beginning of August 1993. It maintained that maternity care should be woman-centred and that choice, continuity and control should be the three main principles at the core of the service to women. It stated the woman must be the focus of maternity care. She should be able to feel that she is in control of what is happening to her and able to make decisions about her care, based on her needs, having discussed matters fully with the professionals involved. It was adopted as Government policy in 1994 and pilot schemes were funded and set up nationwide.

So with Government backing and women, midwives and other health professionals on board one would think that the maternity services would be womencentred offering informed choice, continuity of care and control to women and that all would be well with the maternity world. However there seemed to be much revisiting of old ground. There were many reports at this time e.g. "Making a Difference" (1999). The Fourth Report to the Committee on Health (2002) gave an update of the situation. This was that the Children's National Service Framework (NSF) was announced in 2001 which had a maternity part with the remit to set National standards of care covering antenatal, delivery and postnatal services. The maternal and neonatal workforce group was set up in 2001 to consider workforce issues, staffing for various models of care and configuration of maternity services. £100,000 capital investment was made to modernise over 200 maternity units. The National Institute of Clinical Excellence (NICE) was asked to provide guidelines for electronic fetal monitoring, induction of labour, Anti D prophylaxis, caesarean section and routine antenatal care. Money was provided for an extra 2000 midwives. However it concluded that although it was safer than ever to have a baby, there were still issues with the quality of women's experiences of childbirth and that there was a need to find and resource newer models of hospital obstetric care.

During this time ARM was continually active and ensuring that its voice was heard on as many platforms as possible. Supervision of Midwives (ARM 1995), and education (ARM 2006) were also addressed. Much had improved but much had not. "Midwifery Matters" (DoH 2007) was a document aimed once more at providing a women-centred quality, safe service by offering informed choice, improved access to services and continuity of care and support, and in 2010 "Equity and Excellence: Liberating the NHS" was published which set out to put patients at the heart of everything the NHS does. The new Commissioning Framework offered the chance for woman-centred care based in the community. ARM (2010) published a lengthy response outlining how the maternity networks could be made to work and suggesting the formation of a bipartite service with a locality based as well as hospital service. It covered funding streams, the idea of midwifery as an autonomous profession, localities, accommodation, safety concerns and litigation, no fault compensation, recruitment and retention amongst other matters. It is not clear whether patient choice improved, but it seems that for many midwives little had. There was little if no increase in autonomy for individuals and the profession overall, working patterns were not conducive to health, understaffing increased stress, bullying and the danger of making mistakes (in a punitive system) and working in large maternity units was not conducive to one to one care. The Birthplace study (2011) compared outcomes for births in different settings for healthy women with a straightforward pregnancy. The results showed that giving birth is generally very safe for healthy low risk women. It was rare to find adverse outcomes for babies regardless of the planned place of birth (4-5 in 1000 births).

After this, and in the context of thc commissioning framework, ARM (2013) decided it was time once again to revisit the ideal situation for women and midwives and produced the New Vision. *"ARM sees the mother-midwife relationship as central to maternity care: ARM's Vision is that services would be funded and organised from the bottom up around individual women and their families and within the communities in which they live. Birth at home or in a local birth centre should be the preferred option for all low-risk women. Community maternity care needs separate funding to promote, enable and support normal birth where possible. Restructuring services to be mother-friendly and midwife-friendly will ease the current shortage of midwives. We fully support the ideals of the National Health Service, publicly funded and free at the point of delivery and we are committed to the implementation of this Vision within the NHS. We fully concur with, 'no decision about me without me' (HM Government, 2010) and believe that midwives are the professionals best suited to helping mothers decide what is best for them and their baby..."*

Unfortunately at this time there were major problems in the NHS. In 2013 the Francis report was published as the result of a public inquiry into the role of commissioning, supervisory and regulatory bodies in the monitoring of Mid Staffordshire Foundation NHS Trust between January 2005 and March 2009. It uncovered a lack of basic care, indifference and a lack of basic kindness in the general wards; system failure of the highest order according to Gerada (2013) the chair of the Royal College of

General Practitioners (RCGP). Also at this time the Report of the Morecambe Bay Investigation (Kirkup 2013) detailed a sequence of serious failures of clinical care in the maternity unit of Morecambe Bay NHS Foundation Trust resulting in avoidable harm including deaths to mothers and babies. It found clear instances of substandard clinical practice amongst midwives, obstetricians and paediatricians, and poor working relationships. One of its 44 recommendations was the need for a national review of the provision of maternity and paediatric care in challenging circumstances. In conjunction, a national protocol should be drawn up that defines the types of unit required in different settings and the levels of care that are appropriate to offer in them.

In March 2015, as part of the NHS Five Year Forward View the major review of the maternity services was announced with Baroness Julia Cumberlege to independently lead the review, working with a panel of experts and representative bodies to assess current maternity care provision and consider how services should be developed in a safe, responsive and efficient manner to meet the changing needs of women and babies. The report was published in February 2016 (The National Maternity Review 2016) and found the quality and outcomes of maternity services have improved significantly over the last decade. However, it also found "significant differences across the country, and further opportunities to improve the safety of care and reduce still births" It says that there are seven key areas that should be prioritised:

1. Personalised care, centred on the women, where they have genuine choice, and unbiased information;
2. Continuity of carer, to ensure safer care based on a relationship of mutual trust and respect;
3. Better postnatal and perinatal mental health care;
4. A payment system that compensates providers for delivering different types of care to all women, while supporting commissioners to commission for

personalization, safety and choice;
5. Safer care, with professionals working together across boundaries:
6. Multi-professional working, breaking down barriers between midwives, obstetricians and other professionals to deliver safe and personalised care for women and their babies.
7. Working across boundaries to provide and commission maternity services

Baroness Cumberlege is currently presenting the report and its findings across the country and ARM were one of the first to welcome her in March 2016. ARM welcomes the report and its conclusions, especially as it seems to be in such accord with our philosophy and previous publications. Being mindful of our aims and objectives, the steering group is planning the future direction of ARM. We are in the process of seeking the views of members past and present and will then plan the way forward. What is certain is that ARM will continue to listen to midwives and women themselves, in order to support midwives both individually and collectively as a profession and encourage and assist them to give women centred care, tailored to the needs of women. For myself, I think that although much has changed in the last forty years, there is still so much work to do and I sincerely hope it doesn't take another forty years.

REFERENCES

The Equal Pay Act 1970 is an Act of the United Kingdom Parliament.

Association of Radical Midwives (1986) *The Vision. Proposals for the Future of the Maternity Services* Ormskirk. A.R.M.

Department of Health (1993) *Changing Childbirth: Report of the Expert Maternity Group* (Cumberlege report) HMSO London.

Friedan, B., (2013) *The Feminine Mystique, Betty Friedan 50 Years* WW Norton & Co. VermontGreer, G., (1970) *The Female*

Eunuch Harper Collins, London Harne, L. (2010) Women's liberation and radical feminism 1970 - early 1980s. *Talk at a* London Feminist Network seminar on Saturday 10 April, 2010

House of Commons (1955-6) Chairman Guillebaud. *The Report of the Committee of Inquiry into the Cost of the National Health Service - The Obstetric Service under the National Health Service* London. H,M.S.O.

House of Commons, (1979 - 80) Chairman R Short. *Social Services Committee, Second Report, Perinatal and Neonatal Mortality.* London. H.M.S.O.

House of Commons, (1991-2) Chairman N. Winterton. *Health Committee, Second Report, Maternity Services* London. H.M.S.O.

Maternity Services Advisory Committee (1982) *Maternity Care in Action, Part 1 - Antenatal Care* London H.M.S.O.

Maternity Services Advisory Committee (1984)_ *Materntiy Care in Action, Part 2 - Care During Childbirth*_London. H.M.S.O.

Maternity Services Advisory Committee (1985) *Maternity Care in Action Part 3 - Care of the Mother and Baby.* London H.M.S.O.

Ministry of Health (1970) Domiciliary Midwifery and Maternity Bed Needs: the Report of the Standing Maternity and Midwifery Advisory Committee (Sub-committee Chairman J. Peel), HMSO, London.

Tew, M., (1990) *Safer Childbirth? A Critical History of Maternity Care* Chapman and Hall. London.

Irene Walton
Midwifery Matters 149 - Summer 2016

Coven contributor

"What Does it Mean to you to be Radical?"
In my life as a woman, a mother and a midwife I have always felt a strong connection with the women through history who stand before us and who suffered and strove to care for each

other and their families in every kind of adversity, and who celebrated and shared with generosity in good times. The "radical" idea in my view then relates to these deep roots of female solidarity and sisterhood also expressed in the view of feminist groups in the 20th century and in centuries prior to that. The recognition that the place of women in society is largely the result of the constraints of our biology which gives power and induces fear, but also increases our vulnerability to restrictions of freedom and agency. The female creative power standing as a challenge to the destruction of the natural world.

The central radical idea or root for me is the autonomy which we should possess as adult human beings over our own bodies. The right to consent to or refuse treatment or relationships, and to be cared for with compassion and justice. The right to be free from the male gaze and male appropriation. As the famous feminist quotation goes "the radical notion that women are people" (Marie Shear 1940-2017).

Katherine Hales.
[National co-ordinator for ARM]
April 2021.

Midwife Voice

L – A long-time ARM member no longer practising - '[I] *joined ARM in 1987, and it was my bedrock through midwifery training, and early midwifery career, and all through my careers. And I'm still a member of ARM. So, radical for me, was going back to the roots of midwifery, going to that grassroots part, feminists being with women, and I had another Damascus moment, when I went to my first home birth as a student midwife. And that's when I knew, I wanted to be community midwife. At that point I hadn't known, but that's where I wanted to go, and then I was ending up being an independent midwife for 17 years, so again, being with women, holding that space, bucking the trend...'*

Midwife Voice

I – A long-time ARM member - '*...I haven't just survived, what will next year be a 40-year career as a midwife, but I've been able to enjoy it, for the most part, you know? I was able to be an independent midwife for 14 years; without ARM, I don't even think I would've stayed in midwifery. I needed it. It's been like my nurturing... and enabled me to nurture what I want, and yeah, I've enjoyed seeing ARM develop. And as you know, political action is important to me. I'm a political person and feminist, and I think I'm quite academic as well, and J**** said 'I'm not academic', but I am, quite academic, so it's interesting that J****'s not academic, me, who says I am academic, but we both get something with the same organisation. Yeah... yeah, it's been completely central to my 40 years as a midwife...*'

CHOICE

A Birth Story - Elective Caesarean Section - 'Maternal Choice'

This was sometimes a challenging situation for me. I had, as an Independent Midwife been employed to support women who knew full well that they would not be having vaginal births. This would be for such medical reasons as Twins, PTSD (Post Traumatic Stress Disorder) after vaginal birth, breech presentation or perhaps, incontrovertible medical reasons like placenta praevia. I say 'incontrovertible', but the first three examples in that list are not; I have supported women to have home births with each of those situations. Most of the time, the decision to have a LSCS (Lower Segment Caesarean Section) had been made, and the woman simply wanted the advantages of continuity of carer antenatally and postnatally. Very occasionally, a woman was not fully informed as to her choices and would go on to choose a vaginal birth instead, the compromise being labouring in hospital close to obstetric services should things change. Being a radical IM, providing that I wasn't too busy, I was very happy to support these women.

The most challenging 'elective' LSCS that I supported, involved a previous client. Jessica was a fit and active woman and had booked to have a home birth with me early in her first pregnancy, going on to have one of the most straight forward water births I ever witnessed. It was only in retrospect that I recognised how fearful her partner had been, his relief post birth was obvious, but to be honest, many men supported their partners despite their fear, respecting their choice. So, I hadn't dwelt on this. I wasn't surprised to be called less than two years later when Jessica was pregnant the second time, booking for another home birth - what we used to call in the NHS community area where I worked previously, *'a gift'*; if there was a birth that would predictably be uneventful medically, this was it and we'd invite students in whenever possible as we could pretty much guarantee a great experience regarding witnessing a normal birth.

We weren't very far into the antenatal period, certainly less than 20 weeks, when I started to notice that Jessica was quieter during appointments, not the bubbling gregarious woman I'd known previously. I was at a loss to put my finger on what the problem was. I didn't have to wait too much longer though, as just after her anomaly scan, whilst discussing the environment of the hospital where she'd had the USS (ultrasound scan), she commented that,

"...it's not such a bad place as I thought." When she'd booked the first time, she had recently lost a parent to cancer in that very same hospital, and quite logically connected hospital to illness, further fuelling her decision for a home birth. For many radical midwives, this very reasoning is why we believe so strongly in home as the place of birth - it's not an illness, just part of life, like death - both these family events have been medicalised and removed from the home. (These days at my age, I am heading for being a 'radical midwife for death' - and I'm not the only one, as the ARM transcripts demonstrate - see midwife L)

"What is it Jessica, what's troubling you?" I couldn't hold back any longer - did she have a problem with me? It is so important to having a trusting relationship between midwife and mother-to-be. It is imperative to work out any problems or admit to needing another practitioner - rare, but I have been both sides of this situation in the past too. After a bit of squirming, Jessica came clean and just blurted it out,

"I want a section this time Lynn...". I think I managed to masterfully mask my real feelings, keeping an open face with an unemotional tone of voice, (only as I was by this time older and

wiser as a midwife), to reply with a simple, *"Why is that then, Jessica?"* because she visibly took a deep breath and exhaled before going on with her explanation, ending with,
"I've been so scared to tell you, but I shouldn't have been Lynn. I should've known that you'd support me whatever I chose." This is indeed pleasing to hear, no matter that my heart is crying inside with what I perceive is going to be a huge mistake. I don't think that I was wrong in this intuitive feeling - however, you could argue that it is a matter of perspective, as when I discharged Jessica from care, discussions and feedback forms confirmed that she was happy with her decision and outcome, even if her midwife felt it was a dreadful aftermath.

Once again I will try to shorten the story, as the point of it has already been made - the woman made a choice, I supported that choice, and she had no regrets - result. Jessica had sustained a small tear at her first birth - just the sort that I had no qualms at all about leaving for the body to repair without suturing; the mother being well and able to follow instructions for ensuring healing. Perhaps I misjudged Jessica? Not really, she was simply a creature of habit and my strong advice to *'keep knees close together as much as possible for the first few days'* as well as usual care of the perineum, was not appreciated as paramount. Every time I'd arrived at her home for daily postnatal visits, she would proceed to sit 'taylor pose' (cross legged) right in front of me, and I would correct her immediately. She always apologised (no need - unfortunately she was reaping the consequences, not me) and sit more appropriately. Her perineum did heal fine, but not as 'perfectly' as it might have, and whilst when I discharged her from care that first time, she did not raise any problems, apparently, as time went on, she just *'never felt the same again... especially during intercourse...'.*

The penny dropped. This wasn't just about Jessica. She loved her husband dearly, and he'd made no secret of the home birth being her choice, and now, in that second pregnancy, *his* fears of further damage to Jessica's body were a big factor. I'll be honest, she never came right out and put it that way. But you know, women often share very intimate details about their sex lives, with their midwives during conversations, and once she opened up to her reasoning for wanting a section for her second birth, I never heard any other reason voiced other than that she didn't want further damage to affect *her* experience of intercourse.

I knew just the obstetrician to refer her to. In reality, most obstetricians won't just give women caesarean sections on request in the NHS, after all, it's not cheap and higher risk - I needed to pick the one most likely. There was one at this hospital with a special interest in mental health issues and particularly Post Traumatic Stress Disorder (PTSD). This wasn't specifically PTSD, however, I knew that this obstetrician would have the most open mind. It was all very straight forward in the end - date booked - and I was content to be support to the couple in theatre for the surgery. Being a fit and healthy woman, Jessica's operation went well - baby was well, and they came home within forty-eight hours.

Of course, that's not the end of the story. Jessica went on to suffer two infections, the first serious and necessitating admission to hospital as an inpatient for a few days on IV medication (a wound infection that opened up the scar despite antibiotics). The second, mastitis that developed the week after this - more antibiotics. It was at least a month postnatal before Jessica looked her bubbly self again. I felt enormously sad about what I witnessed, but accepted it.

I'm radical - I support women's choice - it doesn't guarantee it's the wisest of options, but it is her choice, not mine.

Midwife Voice

U - A midwife ARM member from Canada – written contribution - '*What is radical midwifery to me? It is going back to birth as normal and being with the pregnant person through the process supporting the client's choices and advocating when needed in a medical healthcare system if one would enter it. Radical midwifery does question the status quo and ask, "why this path is being suggested?"*

when it comes to medical interventions and suggests less medicalized interventions if available. Radical midwifery educates and informs about normal pregnancy and health and discomfort management for labour and birth...'

Midwife Voice
G - A midwife no longer practising - *'so radical for me is a truth seeker, is a questioner, is an ambassador, is an advocate. Is somebody who for their own self-worth, doesn't take 'that's how it is' as law...'*

Midwife Voice
A - A student midwife - *'...I think it's having the courage to follow one's wisdom of the heart, and to be the advocate for the women we're supporting. So sometimes, it's making difficult decisions and perhaps going... pushing boundaries of policies and guidelines.'*

A Birth Story - Freebirth

I had booked Tania for a home birth when she was only eight weeks pregnant. It was her first baby and she knew what she wanted - a natural home birth, but was well informed enough to know that the NHS in her area could not guarantee this. In reality, no NHS Trust can guarantee this; we have the right to decline what the NHS offers us, but we do not have the right to demand anything (the law, as I understood it, states that Trusts only had to provide 'a maternity service', not specifically what that service should offer). Tania was already part of some online mother/birth discussion groups (the early days - remember Yahoo?) and was aware of the shenanigans that some community areas engaged in. Listening to other mothers' stories, she understood that in attempts to gain trust from women, some midwives would agree to a home birth. But as they worked in teams, not everyone was always on board with the idea of a first timer giving birth outside of an obstetric unit. This plan could be thwarted, often at the last minute. Raised blood pressure was a favourite late development that ensured that a woman was frightened enough to change her mind and 'sensibly', give birth in hospital, *'just in case'*.

Tania was an accountant - she liked numbers, and happily pored over statistics, her analytical mind understanding the mathematical patterns that could be used to demonstrate almost anything. She was a formidable young woman, independent and clearly the lead in her partnership with the father of her baby, who was supportive in all that Tania decided - as it should be; her body, her choice. Whilst I shared pretty much every bit of thinking Tania held on matters of birth, I still had to work quite hard to win her confidence. With mutual respect, we eventually, had a great working relationship - I was clear that I was there to serve her, and she was clear on her choices.

As we approached the last weeks of her pregnancy, Tania began to talk about 'freebirthing'. This is the term used by women who plan to birth without the supervision or aid of a medical professional. She repeatedly stated her belief in the female body to give birth unaided, that if healthy, all a woman needed was privacy. I knew what was coming - I was being tested. It wasn't the first or the last time that I, as an independent midwife, attracted a woman whose heart was willing to freebirth, but whose head would not let her. In keeping with the social norms of modern obstetric thinking, she could not let go of the *'just in case'* mentality. I have always been clear in my own thinking on this matter - 1. If there is any doubt at all, then a woman should not freebirth. In my experience, the women who choose this option and succeed, are complete believers in the natural process and prepared to take full responsibility. - 2. Being afraid to go into hospital, or not trusting NHS staff is not a good reason to birth alone. These women inherently do not believe in the ideology of freebirthing - they're just more afraid of medical care than nature.

So I wasn't surprised when Tania laid out her birth plan, that she did not wish to have the baby monitored, that she would labour in a room alone and that she wanted me to sit in the lounge with her partner (and mother, it turned out) whilst she birthed. Initially, this feels like rejection, not on a personal level, but on the idea that a midwife is needed at all at birth. Her reasoning was that should something go wrong, I could swing into action and save the baby... or her. I pointed out to her how irrational this was, not to mention unfair. A midwife's skills are based in the normal. Through monitoring (sometimes purely via observation), I would be prepared for any deviation from normal, prior to an emergency, so that no heroics (or paramedics and doctors) would be needed.

Tania was adamant about what she wanted, testing my belief that I supported women's choices - whatever they were. In the end, it came down to a matter of responsibility. I also believed in her ability to birth without care or intervention; she was healthy, and the pregnancy had gone well. But it wasn't that simple. Despite being independent of the NHS, in any adverse incident, my care and notes would be scrutinised, every word. I would need to be able to demonstrate that I had 'warned' the woman of all the things that could go wrong... in an adverse incident. Whilst I was utterly confident in Tania's ability to have such a birth, without incident, I also happened to be a Supervisor of Midwives at the time, and our role was to ensure protection of the public through supporting midwives in challenging situations. Whilst I was cool with this scenario, I needed to 'tick the boxes' and engage with the local Supervisory process, just to prove that Tania, and I, knew what we were doing.

Often in these circumstances, Supervisors would want to (insist on) meeting the woman. I was wise to this as just an opportunity to do a bit of shroud waving, so made sure that Tania knew she didn't have to agree to such a meeting. I was not going through this exercise just to cover my arse - no. Supervision no longer exists in this way, but at the time, I believed that when it was used judiciously, I, as an Independent Supervisor of Midwives, could support any other midwife (NHS or independent) in these out of the ordinary situations, enabling them in turn, to support a woman who was wanting to apply her choice and right to this hugely important time of her life.

So, what happened at the birth? It truly was bizarre sitting in the living room with a hyper-anxious granny to be and a gentle quite man, listening to a woman labouring in the bathroom. Tania didn't want a water birth so had not got a pool, but was happily using her little bath to soothe the contractions. The dad to be was intermittently knocking the door (he'd had strict instructions on how often he could do this to offer food and drink) and came out at one point to say that Tania had requested that I come in - she was pushing. I'd done my best to prepare for any scenario, and Tania had been clear, that whatever happened, she wanted to be the first person to handle her baby.

I entered the tiny bathroom without any equipment, not even a Pinard. Everything was set up in the other room. Not just in case, but I would need some things like instruments to cut the cord and so on, and Tania was happy for post-natal observations to be performed. This was all I normally would have had out, including emergency equipment. Once I was in the bathroom, door shut behind me, Tania shouted,
"...it's coming...the baby's coming..." between involuntary pushes. I stood, arms firmly folded, my armpits squeezing my hands to remind me not to touch the baby - it had to be Tania, but I encouraged her to just carry on - she was doing brilliantly.
"... but the water... it's coming...". She had a point - it wasn't that she hadn't planned a water birth - I'd been with many women birthing in baths before birth pools were widely available, no, the problem was that it was very shallow; the baby needs to remain below the surface until fully born. Laying on her back, Tania was bobbing her bottom in and out of the water, having been surprised at the speed of labour. As she was in slight shock, she didn't want to get out, not that there was room, and we would've had to have joined the 'listening party' in the other room. So I just observed, encouraging Tania to concentrate on only keeping her hips under water - her body was doing all the work perfectly well.

As the baby emerged, I watched as it began to break the surface,

"Now, Tania. Pick up the baby... it's there."

"No... I can't... you do it...". No. I wasn't having this. I knew that Tania's greatest wish was to be the first to handle her baby. I refused.

"No, Tania - you must lift the baby...NOW!" I don't think I shouted, but I definitely directed her strongly. As I have found over the years, when a woman trusts her midwife, she actually does what is asked, without question. This is the most useful aspect of knowing a woman in labour. Having formed a relationship, in any sort of emergency (which this wasn't really - I was just being cautious) the woman does what is needed. So many times in hospital births, I've seen emergency care delayed as professionals must spend the time informing the woman of why they need to do what they need to do. Mostly, there is time. But occasionally, there isn't.

She did pick up her baby - all was well. When I discharged her from care, Tania said,

"I'm so glad you made me pick up my baby. I would have been forever disappointed if you had touched her first...". Indeed. I knew this. We women can be complicated in our choices. I would have been the same.

POWER

Coven contributor

Exploring the roots of anything is vital to understanding the 'fruits' and working out how to make change. My approach to learning and teaching has always been to start with the roots. To first ask what underlies the practice, theory, or belief? Where and when did it emerge? What conditions nurtured it? For example, the only way to make sense of common practices in the maternity system is to understand the herstory they emerged from. Practices are not woman-centred or evidence-based because the maternity system has its roots in misogyny and the medicalisation of women's bodies. Practices continue to reflect the notion that women's bodies are dirty and broken and require science and technology to make them safe and efficient. Until these foundational beliefs change, the fruit will remain the same. If we are to change the birth culture, we must take radical action to pull out the roots and plant and nurture new ways of understanding. New ways of knowing need to centre women, and as a midwife, 'with woman' underpins all aspects of my work. If I am unsure, I come back to these roots and ask myself, 'what does 'with woman' look like in this context'? This question can be applied to a range of settings and situations, from midwifery practice with an individual woman to the design of a research project.

As a noun, the word radical refers to a person who holds extremist convictions and principles. However, what constitutes extreme varies depending on the cultural norms of society—for example, challenging a maternity system rooted in misogyny is often considered alternative and extreme. For me, this aspect of being radical has always been an external perception of what I do and say, rather than an internal feeling about who I am. It is also about a way of being in the world that is not aligned with expectations of how a female should behave. As a child, my father encouraged me to question authority, speak the truth and (literally) fight bullies. I was taught that confrontation and disagreement were not something to be afraid of, and that 'doing the right thing' was more important than fitting in. Although this behaviour is admired in boys, it was considered aggressive and difficult in a girl.

My childhood provided the roots for my radical approach to midwifery, and as a midwifery student, I continually questioned what I was seeing. I realised that woman-centred, evidence-based practice was not the cultural norm in maternity care. In my attempts to make sense of this and find my path through it, I came across the Association of Radical Midwives and joined their email forum. I felt a sense of relief that I was not alone and gained so much knowledge and strength from the radical wise women and their online discussions. The group enabled me to experience an alternative and woman-centred philosophy and approach to practice. I was motivated to keep going and become a midwife to make a difference for individual women and advocate for changes in the maternity system.

However, being radical is not comfortable or easy. Women are physiologically and socially primed to respond to a threat by fitting in and fawning. Horizontal infighting is common and solidarity rare within the birth world. Confrontation and disagreement can be met with silencing and suppression rather than debate. For me, being radical often means being misunderstood. People assume that I don't care what others think or don't care about being liked. However, being radical is about choosing between being liked by many or being true to myself. It means having a few people who love and support me for who

> I am rather than lots of people liking me for who I pretend to be. Being radical means not attaching my worth to people's opinions of me. Although it is often difficult to do, it is also freeing to speak the truth and be radically myself.
>
> **Rachel Reed**

A Birth Story - Some Babies Need Special Care

Many of my NHS colleagues believed that all my clients as an independent midwife (IM), were middle-class, 'well-off', as they were paying for my services. I could write a whole chapter on this subject alone, about 'what is a midwife's care of mother and baby over ten months or so, worth?' But I'll stick to what's pertinent here, the perception of my clients by others. There's no doubt that some healthcare practitioners enter the world of private medicine for monetary reasons, but when I was an IM, as far as I could see, we were all practising outside of the NHS for ideological reasons. This meant that I was open to negotiation regarding payment - the key factor being, did they value me and what I was offering? People are very happy to pay solicitors three figure sums for letters on headed paper, and for a medical comparison, the cost of care from me over ten months (no limitations on time spent with client during appointments or labour and birth) was about half the cost of breast implants at the time. I had been paid in kind on occasion as well as having clients pay over a year or more for my services, meaning that women could receive care outside of the NHS on their terms. This set up a feeling of mutual respect. Such flexibility enabled women from all backgrounds, with all situations to access care from me as an IM.

Unexpected Special Care

One very different client was in her early twenties, and worked in the beauty industry. She was married and living in a tiny starter home, 'the best they could afford', who likened me to the sort of midwife one of the celebrities in Hello or OK magazines had for their births - 'private'. For Charlene and Steve, that meant 'the best'. This was a young couple with aspirations, looking to the world of celebrity for pointers on how to live their lives. For example, they bought their push chair/car seat for the baby after seeing Jamie and Louise Redknapp using a particular brand. It mattered to them. To my mind, they were down to earth, ordinary people and I liked them immediately. One element that was, however, different to any other client - she was the only client I ever had who was a smoker.

I of course gave her information to assist her with her desire to give up smoking; she'd already had a miscarriage before, always a high risk for smokers. She did cut down, and eventually gave up, but her pregnancy was already affected; at her 20-week scan, the baby showed inadequate growth. I referred her to an obstetrician who knew me and my practice, and we adopted a shared role, initially simply monitoring growth. Whilst it was not obvious abdominally on palpation at 20 weeks, by 28 weeks, she was barely palpating as 24-26 weeks gestation. Scans were monthly, and as long as the baby continued a reasonable amount of growth, the plan was to 'wait and see'. In fact, by 32 weeks, growth was becoming imperceptible to me, so scans measuring bone lengths were sought, to measure more accurately.

As an IM, I was well aware of the research that demonstrates how poor ultrasound scans are for monitoring growth, however, I trusted this obstetrician, he did all the scans himself, so there was continuity of operator, and he was supportive of me continuing care for the recommendation of a hospital birth for this increasingly vulnerable baby. The only issue we needed to discuss with the parents, was how long could we wait, and from my point of view, was induction of labour (IOL) a good idea at all? In my experience, baby's in trouble in the womb, tend to evict themselves, knowing that they will do better on the outside than inside. (Hence the opposite truism I held, that 'posh babies', stayed in the womb well over their due dates as they were so comfortable - less likely to suffer nutritional deficiencies or toxins). In the end, the parents weighed up everything for themselves, and agreed to a 34 week IOL, rather than the immediate 32 week one as suggested by the obstetrician. He was satisfied that should things deteriorate quickly, I would be recommending IOL sooner - we had a working relationship based on respect and trust.

The date was set, but Charlene was already becoming more and more uncomfortable, the Braxton Hicks contractions starting to look suspicious in my eyes.

"You may not need this induction of labour after all Charlene," I asserted, and also reassured her that usually, such premature labours were comparatively quick; nature seems to know that a compromised baby won't do terribly well in a long and difficult labour. But Charlene got to the induction day, albeit after a horrendous night where she called me for reassurance.

We met bright and early at the labour ward, Charlene looking distinctly uncomfortable. We were welcomed and had a midwife allocated to us; as it was technically an obstetric case, not midwife-led, I was pleased to have another practitioner familiar with all protocols etc, to lead the induction, and I assisted. We all got on well immediately, a positive experience, which was the exception rather than the rule for me as an IM when in an NHS hospital situation. The plan, as Charlene was a primip (first time mother), was to begin with prostaglandin gel to soften the cervix, with an expectation of the usual two doses before being ready to proceed to syntocinon infusion. I discussed with the midwife how we thought that in the light of Charlene's weeks of discomfort, that it was not likely that she would need much in the way of stimulation to get going. First things first, CTG monitoring (continuous tocograph – the machine that records and prints out the baby's heart and mother's contractions), then if all was well, go ahead with a vaginal examination (VE) and administer first suppository.

All was well, in fact, more than well, Charlene's discomfort registered as regular contractions immediately. As expected, the baby was ready to be born. We were delighted. Whatever happened now, we knew that the baby had also chosen that day to be born. The midwife examined Charlene, and found that she was fully effaced and the cervix was beginning to dilate. I tentatively suggested that perhaps we could just continue, let nature take its course, but Charlene was 'primed' mentally to go ahead with an induction, and it was enough that the baby was in tune with things. One suppository was plenty - Charlene gave birth in less than six hours - vaginally without assistance, and the baby was well, no need to rush to SCBU. And the weight? The obstetrician was only 10g out! As he said to me - he agreed that USS were rubbish at assessing big babies - fat was impossible to assess. However, skinny babies are being assessed on bone measurements alone, there is accuracy - with continuity and expertise. I couldn't disagree this time.

But that's not the end of the story. A 34-week baby with normal growth and development rarely needs any special care, it's simply a matter of feeding. But this tiny scrap, not even 2kg, needed some close monitoring at the very least. Charlene was able to reside in the unit with the baby, and had chosen to bottle feed (one of only two of my clients who ever did from birth), which meant that the SCBU staff were highly delighted with the ease of measuring feeds. (This is not the place to discuss pros and cons of this approach... suffice to say, it wasn't what I recommended). Charlene had to vacate her room after a few days, as the unit became busy, but she arrived each day before breakfast and didn't leave until nearly midnight, meaning that only one feed was being administered by staff.

Charlene and Steve lived a fair distance from the hospital, and after a few days of this, I could see her tiring. I enquired to how the baby was doing. It was in a normal cot, not receiving any medications, they just wanted it to 'fatten up a bit', like it was a Christmas turkey. I recommended to Charlene that she take baby home, she was more than capable of monitoring the feeding, and I could visit daily. But owing to previous experiences of SCBU, I decided to test the waters myself first.

"Doctor, what do you say to parents who want to take their babies home from SCBU against medical advice?" I visited Charlene whilst she was at the hospital each day to support her, so I was able to catch the doctor (a Registrar - so very experienced paediatrician) and get an idea of how Charlene's decision to take the baby home would be treated.

"Oh, they don't." The doctor sounded confident. I assumed that he had misunderstood me.

"No, what I mean is, they tell you that they're taking the baby home... today, what then?"

"I tell them that their baby will die if they take it home... and then they don't do it." He actually said this with a grin on his face. I quickly recovered my disgust at his answer, smiled sweetly and then went to let Charlene know. What I told Charlene was that the doctor clearly was not making decisions based on the baby's needs, but his own ego and power to control parents. I offered to tell the staff that she was taking baby home, and that I would continue care.

We did it... a bit of fuss, a bit of bother... but they also knew that the baby was fine. The baby gained weight beautifully at home and just as important, the parents also thrived.

Midwife Voice

Q - A midwife member - *'I started realising that we are going through, I mean we're always going through change. We're always in a sort of dynamic equilibrium aren't we, in terms of women and birth and everything? But there's a definite sea change towards patriarchy that's aggressive right now, that's becoming a wee bit... it's building momentum, and it has echoes. Everyone's right today - it has echoes of the witch hunt...'*

A Birth Story - Surprising Special Care

Lizzie was typically the sort of client people expect IMs to have; an educated, professional career woman, in a stable relationship, having her first baby in her late 30s. She was healthy, but even I became concerned about her blood pressure (BP) by mid pregnancy. In the end, it proved to be more than just pregnancy induced hypertension (PIH), blood results demonstrating mild to moderate pre-eclampsia, the only cure, birth. The aim is always to get to term if possible, weighing up the risks to the baby being born prematurely with the risks to the mother of continuing the pregnancy. The baby was growing surprisingly well, not always the case for pregnancies with raised BP. But at 34 weeks, Lizzie spontaneously laboured, and the baby was born quickly, but not in the best condition. As so often is the case, nature decided that a baby would do better outside the womb, than inside. He was in the SCBU for a week or so before he really stabilised and Lizzie could take over the bulk of care and feeds. Luckily she lived close to the hospital in this case, and it wasn't that onerous. However, being a woman used to 'being in charge' of her life, she began to question if the baby really needed to remain in the hospital. I couldn't disagree, no medications or special care, just lots of 'obs' (observations).

Knowing the hospital and staff (not in a good way), I called to speak to the Supervisor of Midwives (SOM) on call. It was a Friday and a bank holiday weekend was just beginning. She was completely supportive, knowing that between the mother and I, the baby was in good hands; if the mother wanted to take her baby home, then it should just be a matter of paperwork. I felt a bit better being supported by a member of the maternity staff, but let me say, SCBU is a world unto itself in most hospitals; their work is mostly highly specialised, critical care of sick infants, not like midwifery care, which even with modern obstetrics, is still mostly about well women and babies. I always said that it was because I cared for healthy babies all the time, that it was easy to spot a baby that was in trouble, but I knew it wasn't going to be that straight forward supporting the mother in this SCBU.

It was far worse than I imagined. Lizzie and I entered the department that afternoon together, and I stood next to her as she informed the Sister in charge that she was taking her baby home, as she was confident in her care and feeding and that she had her own midwife visiting daily.

"I know it's probably against medical advice, but if you just want me to sign something, that's fine." If only it were that easy.

"I'll have to inform the Registrar on call first..." and the Sister raced off. Minutes later the Registrar arrived, a really lovely doctor, smiling and offering his hand to shake. He was a locum as it was a holiday weekend. He studied the notes and agreed, there wasn't a problem as far as he was concerned. Phew. But the Sister (in charge... as I said) decided that as he was a locum, that she should call the Consultant. Really? On a bank holiday weekend? But I was underestimating the territorial culture. Midwives did not dictate when babies were well enough to go home - the locum wasn't really 'one of them' poor man, he was caught in the middle.

What ensued, was a gathering. The Consultant didn't waste time, he arrived to assert authority over the wayward locum and rogue midwife, barely acknowledging the mother - the person in the room who actually, had the absolute legal right to do want she wanted with her baby. The Sister joined us and proceeded to inform the Consultant that in her opinion, the baby wasn't ready to go home,

"Perhaps after the holiday weekend?" she said. I should have known. It was an administrative issue; the NHS is a 24/7 service that falters every time the office workers aren't at their desks. The locum was out of his depth, the Consultant sat opposite me, once again ignoring the mother, and asked me,

"Who's your manager?"

"I don't have a manager. I'm an independent midwife."

"You must have someone in authority over you...?" He had no idea.

"Well, there are Supervisors of Midwives in every area on call." I offered, wondering what on earth was the difference that he thought it would make.

"Who's that here then?"

"It's Carol Smith - I spoke to her earlier. She's in agreement with us. The baby will be fine at home."

"Carol Smith? She's just a community midwife...!" He was incredulous. He couldn't understand how Supervisors worked as a support, and therefore could come from any area of midwifery - sometimes even teachers. "I'll call the Head of Midwifery, Jane, she'll soon sort you out."

"I'm not an employee of the Trust, so she doesn't have any authority over me." I may've smiled. There is essentially no hierarchy in the midwifery profession - (in theory) we are all equal, not like in nursing, but the NHS has its own hierarchies, regardless. My smile perhaps riled him somewhat, as he didn't stop there.

"If you continue with this course of action, I will have no choice but to call the Police." I was certain he was bluffing - scare tactics - not quite as unforgivable as shroud waving, but still bullying. I simply reiterated that I would support my client's decision.

"Then you give me no choice...". I won't deny, I was frightened. It was the way he threatened, the piercing stare at me, the confident swagger - I was nothing to him. At that moment my client, Lizzie, the mother of the baby, jumped out of her chair and stood next to me.

"Don't you dare threaten my midwife like that." I was horrified that it had come to this. A new mother feeling the need to defend her midwife. But all he'd done was harden her resolve that she was doing the right thing. After all, the other doctor, hadn't seen a problem - and he was clearly a decent human being compared to this man.

Lizzie got her baby home. No, he didn't call the Police - I knew it was a bluff. But, he did call Social Services - a holiday weekend, he called our over stretched NHS Social Services to justify his behaviour, and basically, just be a bastard. I got a call from a very confused social worker that night. They had the details of the family, but of course this was the first time they'd ever had contact with Social Services - no history, and as far as the social worker was concerned, with another Health Professional (me) visiting daily, where on earth was the risk? What a waste of everyone's time. She was apologetic - I was apologetic - why were we all apologising for the behaviour of a Consultant paediatrician with an ego the size of the hospital? Of course nothing ever came of it, but I vowed that I wouldn't ever get to the point of a client having to support me again - I was the one that had to remain strong. But I was very proud of Lizzie.

Midwife Voice
L – A long-time ARM member - no longer practicing - '*okay... so radical for... my background - I called myself a radical feminist in the late 70s early 80s, and I came to midwifery through feminism. Basically... had a kind of epiphany roundabout 80-81, that I wanted to be a midwife and followed that through. I mean, when I was a nurse in the olden days, and at the end of my training, I was told I was a nonconformist by my set tutor... "...you know, A****, you're a non-conformist, stay like that". So I did kind of buck the trend...*'

A Birth Story - Expected Special Care

Clara was a second time mum, her first an emergency caesarean section for pre-eclampsia at 34 weeks. I cannot reveal the ultimate reason for Clara wanting an independent midwife as it was so unique, that it would be identifying and break with confidentiality. However, it was not a medical reason. As expected, Clara developed high blood pressure very early on. She was thankful of having an IM in the end, for the added bonus of my daily visits which enabled her to remain at home and not need to be an inpatient. Meanwhile, I was able to liaise with her obstetrician. With a toddler at home, this working mother, a fit and otherwise healthy woman was delighted to be able to minimise disruption to her family right up until the day of the planned LSCS at 34 weeks. She had required medication for the bulk of the pregnancy, just to get that far.

The surgery was uncomplicated, and the baby did well in the

SCBU for the first week. Whilst the baby remained well, Clara an experienced breastfeeding mum of a premature baby previously, just got on with expressing and feeding. Unfortunately, there was an outbreak of MRSA (Methicillin-resistant Staphylococcus aureus) on the unit and Clara's baby tested positive. Clara was immediately blamed as the culprit and put with her baby in isolation. However, Clara turned out to be negative. After a couple of days of isolation, being left alone to get on with baby care, staff reluctant to interact, Clara called me to say that she had decided to take her baby home. I wasn't surprised, this confident woman was more than capable of doing what was needed.

"Would you like me to come in to support you, whilst you speak with the staff?" Whilst a different hospital to my previous negative SCBU experiences, I knew my role and wasn't going to shy away.

"Oh no, Lynn, that's fine. Hubby will be here in a minute. I'm just packing my things up. I've left a note in the cot telling them I've gone home."

I so wished I'd been a fly on the wall to see their faces when a woman exercised her right to walk out of hospital with her baby. Apparently, a midwife ran down to the entrance where Clara was waiting for her husband to arrive. The midwife was brandishing forms for Clara to sign. She declined... That's a strong woman.

VOCATION

Coven Contributor

As I recline here lazily on my bed contemplating your question my mind fills with myriad memories and also reflections. In the background I have a reminder voice that I am on call for a home birth back up and should go and do some bits and pieces like shower and eat in case I get called out. That reminder voice is easily subdued as having breakfast is the least of my priorities as yet.

My instincts are telling me I shall not get the phone call to be the second today. This reminds me of conversations I've had with many other radical midwives. We tend to know when the calls are likely to come. None of us have ever come to a clear conclusion of why we know this. Many great stories abound amongst us demonstrating this common experience. Is it an ancient wisdom and energy passed on to us? What others may perceive as a type of witchcraft? A type of knowing.

Has anyone done the RCT?

My instincts have guided me all my life and led me to the UK Association of Radical Midwives.

Firstly though, I was surrounded by childbirth, being one of seven children. It was a mysterious but ordinary and joyful event in my family. However, looking after children and making ends meet was far less joyful for my post World War Two traumatised parents. They sent us off to Catholic schools where the nuns presented their version of the world which had many elements of cruelty about it. Then in the seventies there was hippies and music and experimentation and I was up for all of it in my young teenage years. At 17 I was pregnant and found one pregnancy advice book to read when I was sent into hiding to save the family shame. I absorbed all the details and knew my body would give birth without any dramas. My 6-hour physiological breech birth of my marvellous daughter happened in 1975. Maybe it was then I realised I had a calling to become a midwife. Even though all went well there was much more my attendants could have done to make it a more respectful and loving and sacred experience.

Becoming a midwife was a bit tricky for me. I became a nurse first in 1977 as there was no direct entry then. I tried in the mid-eighties but my feminist approach did not match the School of Midwifery I was attending so we parted ways. It was then I first heard of the existence of the Radical Midwives. But they were in the northern hemisphere and I was in the Southern Hemisphere! (No World Wide Web then!)

Then, by some twist of fate through falling in love with an Englishman called Michael, I ended up in Nottingham and along the way met my dear friend Andrea who said how she was off to be a midwife. This was in the early 1990's. It was my reminder call and it felt obvious that I would try again. So that's what I did and I qualified in 1994. Nottingham midwifery lecturers were such a gift to me as too were my kind and loving mentors. We all remain in touch to this day. I was a noisy challenging bolshie feminist Australian which they cleverly translated into being 'passionate'.

This passion brought me finally into the arms of ARM in December 1994. It was Xmas and the meeting was in London. Suzanne Colson brought her entire family along to sing carols in French. Caroline Flint was there sharing her ideas about continuity as well as so many more marvellous strong opinionated passionate radical midwives. They believed in women having choices and being able to birth well, undisturbed wherever they chose with respectful loving midwives, even much better if they knew you. Radical midwives knew this would give them the best chance to be with their babies in a joyful loving way which would be the best start in life for them and their families.

We also knew, as Mary Cronk would remind us, 'some births need help' and we wanted those advanced skills to assist if necessary. There were hints of midwives being in trouble as they transgressed unnecessary rules, but the ARM was there to care and share and support them. Much of the mainstream didn't seem particularly interested in our approach. Along the way I met Lynn Genevieve too and am very happy to have kept in contact to hear about her travels in midwifery too and to be in her 'coven'.

Also being a radical midwife means you can sing feminist songs in your loudest voice like 'Shameless Hussies', drinking wine and eating vegetarian feasts at the seasonal meetings and the Retreats.

The structure of ARM was apparently simple, yet very complex at times – that is another story.

Being a radical midwife commits you to working with women 'where they are at'. It means supporting and attending home births. It means being under the radar sometimes and happily promoting physiological birth and challenging harmful behaviours in the hospital system. It means finding kindred spirits you can work with. It means finding and fighting for the evidence that supports best practice. It means trusting in human birthing processes that work well. It is also about understanding that nothing is perfect and sometimes more help is needed or when nothing can be done.

When my daughter Leif also trusted in birthing (probably by osmosis) and was not comfortable with the idea of hospitals 'as they were for sick people' chose to give birth at home in 1999 she asked me to be her radical midwife for the birth of her son, my grandson Linus. Some were concerned and predicting dire consequences and even attacked me and calling me a 'witch'. Scorn would not stop Leif nor this radical midwife and she gave birth powerfully. We have such a special healing family memory forever.

There is a river of confidence in knowing that there is what I call ancient energies that support you in your work but also that you need a deep, ever developing knowledge and skill set to have the privilege to attend any woman giving birth. You must also take care of yourself so you can bring your settled being to the birth and to know when to stop if you are too tired and unfocused. It means recognising that energies wax and wane like the moon and responding to this. Also, to know you will unknowingly offend many just by your presence. In this way ideas become stronger in your understanding. This means sharing the stories and the wisdom and support and love and the strengthening in the radical midwifery-hood.

Kerri-Anne Gifford

Breeches

Breech babies pitch up in around 4% of pregnancies, more often in twins, but my records show that 10% of the births I attended whilst independent were breech. This higher than average figure came about as once you are known to have the rare (these days) skills, you are sought out by the brave women wanting to birth their babies this way rather than accept the most offered solution in hospital of a planned caesarean section. I do not say brave because having a breech baby at home is especially high risk requiring courage, but brave in going against the grain, against medical advice, in challenging a system that does not inherently trust a woman's body to birth without intervention. That's what takes real guts, being able to sit in a doctor's office and say,
"Thank you for your advice doctor, but I'm going to have my baby in the safety of my home with the midwife." And to be able to say this just after you've been told that unless you have a caesarean section in hospital your baby is likely to die. My wonderful mentor, the woman who taught me how to help women birth their breech babies, Mary Cronk MBE, also taught me to encour-

age women to believe in the safety of their home to birth. Whilst we midwives can be seen as strong women, I always felt this was a myth. I was only as strong as my clients; if she was strong, then I could be strong for her. Sometimes it was just fortuitous that a client already booked with me happened to end up presenting at term as a breech. This was the best case scenario as there was already history between us either by virtue of previous babies or simply our developing relationship antenatally.

One of my regulars, Gail, (she had three babies at home with me as her midwife in the end) presented with breech for her second. In that case, given the option to consult with an obstetrician she elected for an ECV, (external cephalic version, the baby turned to the more common head presentation). When the baby flipped back around soon afterwards, she decided to go ahead with another home birth, and the obstetrician was supportive. As I regularly referred women to him, we had a good working relationship; I trusted his skills, and he trusted mine. My client had another gentle home birth.

A Birth Story - Planned Breech Labour

Women were increasingly seeking me out as a practitioner who would support breech birth, as opposed to breech delivery or elective caesarean section for breech. Some arrived incidentally as I said, often the case with women expecting twins booking with me. My mentor Mary Cronk was an absolute legend regarding breech births. Once, with another client, Emma, I rang a labour ward of a local Trust just as a courtesy as she was in labour nearby; you hope not, but you may need them later - I wasn't to know that in this case I would. I asked to speak to whoever was in charge that day.

"Hello, my name's Lynn Walcott. I'm an independent midwife and I'm with a client in your area. I'm just ringing to say that she's in labour and it's a breech, first baby." The sharp intake of breath on the other end was audible.

"Are you coming in for a section then? We're not busy, I can have theatre ready in a jiffy."
"That won't be necessary, she's planning to birth at home." I paused to let the fact of the matter sink in, the decision was the woman's where and how she chose to birth.
"Oh..." I could feel the co-ordinator's fear through the phone line. I felt a little mean stringing her along like that. But I always enjoyed the punch line,
"I have Mary Cronk with me. I'll only ring again when the baby is born or if we need to come in." This time there was a long sigh, a relaxed, out breath,
"Oh, okay then. No worries with Mary there. Have a lovely baby...". It was like a charm, dropping Mary's name like that.

This time we did need to go in for a caesarean in the end. As was most common in a breech baby that couldn't be born this way, the labour stopped, the woman's body sending a strong message of, *no - this isn't going to work this way*. At least she tried and knew that it wasn't to be and wouldn't always wonder if she would have been able to birth vaginally if she'd had a planned section. With a halted labour, there is no rush, and we lazily made our way to the labour ward after alerting them to our need to transfer in. I must tell of the poor, young, junior doctor sent to admit us in triage. He had no idea why we were there, all part of the training, he has to learn to ask the right questions and report back to the Registrar on duty. It was going so well, then when he asked what had brought us in as she obviously wasn't labouring, I casually said,
"Emma's membranes ruptured yesterday but she hasn't gone in to labour... it's a breech... so...". I wasn't able to finish before, bless him, he'd jumped up to press the emergency bell whilst uttering,
"Oh my God..." and starting to prep the woman verbally for an emergency section.... He clearly didn't have a clue why we were all so serene with this scenario.
"Well, doctor, the baby hasn't attempted to arrive for the last eighteen hours, so I doubt it's about to make an appearance in

the next few minutes." I reassured, trying not to smirk.

A Birth Story - Unplanned Breech Labour

I am not afraid to admit, that I once had an undiagnosed breech - it can happen to anyone. Faye was to be a VBAC (Vaginal Birth After Caesarean) and had a slow beginning of labour, which was unusual for a VBAC in my experience. After a night and day with no apparent change, I offered a VE (vaginal examination), and there it was, a bottom – she palpated as head down, or so I thought. As Mary Cronk had taught me, a breech labour that doesn't progress is safest born by LSCS. You just don't mess around trying to push a breech through a pelvis; if it wants to be born that way, it will be. We transferred in... and actually, there is a bit more of that story to tell.

It was a hospital that I'd never needed to go in previously, despite having births in the area. So they were terrified of me, I think. Certainly, they felt it necessary to call out the SOM (Supervisor of Midwives) to attend when I arrived. What was rather funny, was that I was wearing a t-shirt a friend had brought back for me from a holiday in America - she'd been to Salem, the notorious town where there'd been a high incidence of witches burned. A picture of a witch on a broomstick was obviously too near the mark for the staff. So probably not the best introduction to their local IM. However, at least we were all in agreement that a LSCS was needed.

At first, they did not want me to be in theatre, but the SOM was at least supportive on that front, and I'm so glad I was present (and maybe, even the staff were?). The surgery was no problem, but the baby was not vigorous at birth. The paediatrician present was very inexperienced. I always feel sorry for junior doctors, at the beginning of their clinical training they are just thrown in at the deep end. The baby began to deteriorate, and whilst the staff midwife in theatre to receive the baby, support the mother, and watch me (my perception) implored the very

young, looking doctor to get on with resuscitation, I stepped in to do just that. I couldn't understand why the midwife herself hadn't just gone ahead, but I suppose it showed the strength of the local hierarchy. This midwife then shouted at me,
"You're not allowed to do anything!" She was horrified that I was 'practising clinically' when I didn't have a contract - I was there only on sufferance and as a moral support for my clients. I just retorted that it was an emergency and got on with what needed doing. The doctor finally came to her senses and took over from me. The babe was fine, just needed a bit of help to get going. Afterwards in the staff room, to her credit, this midwife did apologise to me. Contract or no contract, in an emergency, I would have been negligent to have not acted.

A Birth Story – Breech Booked In Labour

Being one of the few practitioners available for breech births, meant that it wasn't unusual to be called when a woman was at term and at the end of her tether. Trying to get the NHS to agree to a natural breech birth was one thing, but for a home birth, nigh on impossible. Mostly it was a case of a hospital Trust just not having midwives with the skills for breech birth. However, they were always happy to pour resources into ensuring midwives were all competent for obstetric skills such as caring for women with epidurals, but breech birth was never a priority. I always tried to get to know the woman a bit before she laboured, which when they were often 36 weeks or beyond, meant a lot of home visits over a short time... if we were lucky. I'd regularly been called as a second midwife to attend a breech birth for a woman whom I did not know - just sensible precautions on the primary IM's part. It wasn't like in the NHS where most home births they insisted on two midwives in case there was an emergency, which virtually never happens with healthy women at term, by the way. But in a breech, it wasn't so out of the ordinary to need to assist the newborn to get going, so another midwife to reassure the mother was normal practice.

I remember Tina extremely well, despite only meeting her for the first time, in labour, with her breech baby, a couple of days after our first conversation. After this one, conversation, she was obviously so relieved to find someone to support her, she'd relaxed enough to go into labour, on the day I'd planned to visit her for the first time. She was 38 weeks and had a birth pool already set up for her originally planned home birth. I have midwifed twins born in water, but never a breech, although plenty had used water for the labour.

It was Tina's first baby, and she had a very straight forward labour and birth - typically quick as most breeches are. She chose to vacate the pool in the end. I always aimed to use these opportunities to train other midwives in breech, and I had another IM who was new in private practice. What was great about this situation, was that technically, I was too far away to provide regular care, so this other IM was able to provide the bulk of the postnatal care. Tina moved house before her next baby was due, and was closer to where I was now living, so booked with me for her second baby and the other IM she knew, was the back up this time. Primarily I always worked alone - having other practitioners involved only for specific situations.

This arrangement was to prove to be so important, when in the last couple of months of Tina's second pregnancy, my personal circumstances meant that I needed to give up her care to the back-up midwife. She was the only client that I ever had to do this for. Tina was absolutely lovely about it - had a lovely home birth with the other IM, but my guilt remained. However, a couple of years later, I 'bumped into' Tina at a midwifery rally outside of the Houses of Parliament! I was there with hundreds on a bitterly cold winter's day, to present a petition to government - and I even stood on a soap box with a megaphone and rallied the crowd - there's a picture somewhere? But Tina was one of the many mothers there to support IM's, and she was so pleased to see me and show off her toddler wrapped up in a sling close to her body. I was apologetic again for letting her down, but she was so generous and kind, that I was finally able to release the guilt. What a gift.

A Birth Story – Freebirthing A Breech

There's another breech that is memorable for unusual reasons. Beth and Peter had a child already, and they were in an area where I wasn't familiar with the local hospital. Her local IM's had declined to take her on, as in her own words,
"...because I am asking too much." This intrigued me. Yes, she was a breech presentation with only a couple of weeks to go, but they were experienced in breech birth too. Basically, she had planned to 'free birth', the situation I'd had previously, but of course, with a breech, the risks are somewhat higher. I agreed to meet. The issue in supporting a woman's choice for me, is always that she is prepared to take responsibility for what she is asking, understands the possible risks, and knows the limitations of the midwife in such circumstances. As long as I consider she is of sound mind, her reasons are her own - although women generally are pleased to share their philosophy of choice.

The couple had done their research and were open to the idea of a transfer in for assistance if the birth was not straightforward, but as with my previous client, just wanted me on site. I went through all the usual contact with the local hospital Trust, liaising with the SOM there, and agreed to care for Beth - but I did have one condition - I wanted to let the hospital know when I was attending her in labour, so that should I call to transfer into hospital, there was no time wasted with information sharing. I reassured Beth, that I would not allow the hospital to bother us - I told the SOM I'd call back once the baby was born. It was all about compromise - but not a compromise of safety. Beth did not want any other practitioner around, so this back up plan, was for a worst case scenario situation. She was a healthy multiparous woman, and I had every confidence that she'd pop the baby out, probably whilst I slept in another room. (I've always been good at sleeping - anytime, anywhere - I'm blessed).

I was trying to demonstrate to her that I trusted her confidence too - that I did honestly believe that she could birth this baby on her own. I managed a couple more visits before she went into labour, and as agreed, Peter showed me into the spare room on arrival, and he and their child retired to their bedroom - Beth was doing her thing in the living room. I made my call to the hospital, and then settled down.

I was woken from a doze by Peter at some point, as Beth wanted me with her - not Peter, just me. They were such a 'together' couple. I never once got any negative vibes off them about the dynamics of our relationships - they just both respected and loved each other, there was complete trust. As I'd agreed, I did not speak, I did not approach until asked. I crouched out of sight, but nearby and waited. I was assessing the situation - and quite typically, she'd called for me during transition. She soon started to involuntarily push. We'd discussed various ideas on breech birth - I'd talked her through my usual care which followed the most common position women adopted to birth - kneeling in various ways at various times. Beth, however, was favouring a deep squat with alternating knee down with each contraction. When after a few contractions, the baby wasn't emerging, I cautiously approached and gently touched Beth on the arm in-between contractions. I had the sonic aid in my hand and without words suggested I have a listen. Beth nodded - and I got a quick reassuring listen to a steady FH before the next contraction.

I went to move away again, but Beth caught hold of my arm and in so doing, found herself having to go onto both knees. Immediately, a foot dropped out of her vagina and got as far as the knee before it stopped at the end of the contraction. She pushed aside my hand as I tried to listen to the FH again. And yet now, she was asking for reassurance.

"Is it ok?" Who knows, I thought?

"It will be." Said far more confidently than I felt. I didn't have any creeping dread or fear though, but I felt handicapped. I was expected to assess the baby's condition without the raft of checks other practitioners use, and even from my point of view, I felt at sea as I'm usually able to watch a labour unfold, watch and know what is happening. I had nothing really to go on and only one FH observation. Just to add to the drama, I was aware of my mobile vibrating constantly - the hospital (surprise, surprise) was not keeping to their side of the bargain, and trying to get hold of me... continuously.

Luckily, nature knew what she was doing, Beth deep down knew what she was doing, and I was able to just then watch as the baby birthed fully in the next contraction - no classic pause between body and head being birthed and that beautiful moment when the baby flexes - nope - just one long smooth exit, into Beth's own hands. I was able to move away again, and watch. She fed the baby quietly until she felt the placenta coming and then invited me to assist and catch the afterbirth in a bowl. Then... at last, she asked that Peter be called in to cut the cord. I could at last put the hospital out of their misery - there were a lot of missed calls!

KNOWLEDGE

Coven contribution

I agree about going back to the "root" and the root for me is the childbearing woman. It involves thinking.. (I love the Midwife Thinking blog.) Thinking "what are we here for?", "what are our aims?" in any situation. Answering that means listening to the woman and pulling on our knowledge and experience. It means being actively involved in the situation, though often this is through quietly waiting as the mother is the central actor, not the midwife. We cannot think out everything from scratch all the time but we have to be alert to each unique situation. This puts us at odds with the system which, in these days of centralised services on an industrial model, seeks to standardise practice through guidelines, policies, procedures and other rules of the game; thus treating women as machines.

Being radical in our sense is also about trust; trust in women, in their bodies and in birth. We are rooted in our knowledge of physiology: how birth works, and the tremendous power of the birthing body and its relationship with the fetus. We gain this knowledge mainly through our experience, rather than our formal education. E.g. seeing how unrestrained women move in second stage to adapt to the position of the fetus and enable its decent. Sadly this is rarely seen in hospitals where women are restrained by equipment and staff expectations and so staff have to be trained in skills and drills for standard "emergencies", rather than helping women avoid these emergencies in the first place. We need to be observant as we watch and listen to women and learn from our colleagues who do this well e.g. Mary Cronk on breech births. Always alert to colleagues' observations which often start with "have you noticed how...?" and followed by what, from other lips, would be seen as an insightful research hypothesis. I think we also have a duty to learn about the aspects of physiology we cannot see: the hormonal feedback systems and epigenetics for example. This is a direct learning from women, rather that the technology driven impetus fuelling so much research.

It is this trust, grounded in our commitment to and love of women and birth and in our ever-increasing knowledge, which means we are not fearful. This is crucial as maternity services are now so dominated by fear: fear of being sued, censured by management or colleagues, not fitting in with colleagues, bullying and tragically fear of birth itself. Fear is contagious and corrosive for workers and childbearing women and currently at epidemic proportions in maternity hospitals. This fear prevents us from learning and leads to the implementation of crude, standardised protective measures against "risk" which cannot work because people are not standardised.

Our trust also prevents us from seeking to control. Which alienates us from the current industrial model which see safety as coming from ever greater control of women, of birth and of those who work with birth.

Birth is the entrance to society and those with power in society have always sought to control birth and therefore midwives: the church, the landowners, the state and now the vested interests of modern capitalism. Implicit in this control is a deep fear of the power of women. There is a long pattern of dominant forces seeking to uproot well-rooted midwives whether by branding them as witches or making sure they "rotate" and don't stay in one place for long enough to really establish local roots.

So, I am a radical midwife and I know where my roots are and where they should be growing. The knowledge I thus gain also highlights where my radicalism departs from and causes problems with the status quo. It was ever thus but the infiltration of the powers that be into the details of practice was never as great as it is now. So being a radical midwife becomes harder and often lonelier, hence ARM.

Mavis Kirkham
Midwifery Professor Emerita at Sheffield Hallam University

Midwife Voice

S - An ARM member who is an antenatal teacher, gave a written answer to the question in a poem -

What radical means to me

Radical is the act of questioning
Radical is the question of 'allowing'
Radical is asking why not,
Radical is not bowing

Bowing to the patriarchal view
That our bodies, minds and souls
Are theirs to protect, administer and govern
To help us remain as dolls

Dolls that look pretty, talk pretty, obey pretty
Dolls that spread their legs
For members, stirrups and scissors
All while lying flat on their bed

Radical means the art of questioning
That's what radical means to me
Radical is saying no, or not now, or wait
Instead of having to plea

I have also used poetry occasionally to share views and experiences of birth and midwifery. Here is a poem I wrote following a workshop at the ARM conference 'Birth in the Balance'. It was accepted for publication in *Lifespan Vol. 1 – Birth* (Pure Slush Books

2021). It is a true account of three generations of my family. I believe that poetry can illicit the pure emotions behind a story.

Birth in the Balance: Grandmother, Mother & Daughter.

Grandmother

It's 1962,
She is 27 and pregnant with her third baby,
and they say "You must have it at home this time."

It's a Monday
in early September,
and the midwife, *Sister Browning says,* "You must wait."

Wait,
waters broken?
She just wants it over.

Friday
she is still waiting,
and *the midwife says,* "Drink this and I'll see you later."

Later?
She has time to scrub the floor then,
on her hands and knees she works, then has a big bowl of mushroom soup.

It's later
and she says, "Husband, get the midwife."
and he leaves to pick up the midwife from her house.

It's a quarter past midnight,
the baby is here, on her due date,
A girl.

Mother

It's 1989,

She is 27 and pregnant with her third baby,
and they say, "You must have it in hospital."

Hospital,
that building full of sick people?
she says, "No, I'm having a homebirth this time."

It's March,
early hours of a Thursday morning,
Her waters have broken.

Later,
she calls the midwife
and Sister Brown arrives soon after.

It's just before nine in the morning,
the baby is here,
another brother for big sister.

Daughter

It's 2012,
She is pregnant with her third child,
She will have another homebirth.

Homebirth,
nice and easy first and second time
with mother, an independent midwife.

Retired now
Mother says, "You'll be fine with the NHS,
you've had two before."

It's October,
late evening,
They said, "Call us when you're in early labour."

She calls,
They say, "You have to come in to the hospital,

we don't have a midwife for you."

Come in,
after two homebirths are they mad?
Her labour stops.

A Supervisor of Midwives calls,
She says, "We will send paramedics,
for the baby's safety if you don't come in."

Safety?
Mother says, "Go to bed daughter, rest,
we'll call them again when the baby's coming."

By morning
she is in labour and in the pool,
the door bell goes.

Husband opens door,
"Hello. Midwives!" *she says*
as she steps, uninvited into the house.

Mother steps forward,
She says, "We haven't called you yet."
the midwife steps past her into the birth room.

Daughter looks confused,
Midwife says, "Hello, what are your contractions doing?"
mother steps forward.

Protective
She says, "Get out!"
how dare they!

Midwife looks at daughter
and says, "You don't want me here do you?"
daughter shakes head.

Midwife turns to mother
and says, "But I was told to rush here."

really?

Mother is incensed
She says, "No-one was interested in rushing to my daughter last night"
she closes the door as they leave.

Later, a kind midwife arrives,
She says, "We're just in the next room if you need us."
she knows the mother and the daughter.

After daughter screams, a final, fearful scream,
The midwife says, "Here's your baby."
it's a girl.

Past, Present, Future,
We say, "Birth in the Balance."
I say, "We must stay Radical."

Lynn Genevieve January 2021
Birth – Lifespan Vol. 1

Midwife Voice

H - An ARM member attending her first national meeting - *'what's the question, how am I radical? Okay, so, I would say I'm not a majorly radical person in a day-to-day basis. But when it comes to midwifery, right from the beginning of my training, the reason I became a midwife, was after my two home births. Having that one midwife who really supported me and kind of connected to me on a real spiritual level during my first birth, and that planted the seed. So, I kind of knew how powerful it could be you know, going through birth, and having that support. And I kind of wanted to help other women in that way. Being in the hospital setting, I knew, was going to be a real challenge during my training, and when I qualified, and I would just do little things that might not seem much, but kind of... always talking about 'birth' rather than 'delivery' and kind of asking the questions and you know? Like I remember one time, a delivery suite midwife, who I think was of many years, and she was like, "first time mum - she's never going to deliver her baby vaginally" and I just* *questioned it. Which at the time was like, ugh! But it felt good... to sort of, make her stop and think, like why was that acceptable to say that anyway? And now, I'm in community, I carry on with being careful about the words I use, and just being mindful, of not getting fully sucked into the system. That how we talk about women, and how we talk about procedures, and how we just accept all these interventions without thinking about them. So, yes... the critical thinking element is important throughout, and I'm just starting my PMA* [Professional Midwifery Advocates] *training, so I hope that I can kind of support midwives even more, to have the confidence to stand up, and stay true to themselves, and you know, get the support they need in this difficult and stressful and challenging job that we all love to do. So yeah, it's kind of my daily attempt to empower women and encourage change in colleagues and sort of, get them thinking about things, and why are we doing it this way? Well, I'm forever emailing the matrons and staff – why we're doing it this way and then I get, "gosh A**** again", you know? So yeah, I think as I get older and I'm less concerned with how people are seeing me, more concerned about staying true to my beliefs, and my thoughts, you know, my ideals and wanting to suck all your knowledge as well, and learn from you guys who've been doing it a lot longer. So yeah, that's... that's my answer.'*

A Birth Story - Vbacs

Vaginal birth after caesarean is much better supported today than when I was practicing. However, the examples I share probably still would be considered too high risk for a home birth. All of these mothers, taught me about the pointlessness of setting limits, as well as the importance of individualised care. All births are unique, but could be put into classifications - in these cases, the only unifying factor is that the women had all had previous caesarean sections. I cannot however say that they were previous 'LSCS' (*lower segment* caesarean sections) - I shall begin with the odd one out; a VBACC (Vaginal Birth After *Classical*

Caesarean).

Hands up who's come across a vertical scar on a woman's abdomen instead of the usual transverse incision - and further, knows that the uterine incision is also vertical - the so called *'classical'* caesarean section? (I've always wondered - is it 'classical' owing to being the original style, or because it was so named for Julius Caesar in a 'classical' period?). Fair to say that in modern obstetrics, it is no longer applied or needed. So why did this woman, Karen have one in the late 1990's for a first baby - and an elective one, not an emergency at all? Basically, it was owing to the presence and situation of fibroids. There was no other safe choice. What a blow to a woman who'd planned a home birth with her first child.

She hired me, an IM for the second pregnancy in full knowledge that the request to have a home birth was going to be a challenging one - even to an IM. She was well aware why incisions are normally transverse and in the lower segment today - and it isn't to hide the scar in a bikini.... With her classical scar inhabiting the upper segment, the part that would be stretching the most in pregnancy, she had been warned that even another pregnancy was a risk, let alone the idea of labouring next time around. When I met her, she had already pretty much done all the research on the subject - there just wasn't any modern cases to learn from - it was a truly unique scenario. The only thing everyone agreed on, was that it was definitely 'a high risk' - and I didn't disagree.

Karen wasn't completely closed to the idea of another caesarean if absolutely necessary, but wanted to be certain that all options had been explored. I could advise on labour and birth in the home environment, particularly to support VBAC in general, but we needed another opinion. Karen was quite happy to speak to an obstetrician about a vaginal birth. I carefully chose the Consultant, one that I knew would understand a woman wanting a normal birth; this obstetrician had given birth at home herself - twice.

The Consultant was great - sympathetic to Karen's desires,

but completely honest about risk - *she just didn't know - couldn't quantify it.* She gave her the low down on the risks for LSCS, agreeing that a VBAC in those circumstances was safe, and wasn't even against home births for them, but for Karen's individual case, we were all in the dark. This is where the importance of a woman's intuition and beliefs come into play. I had found over the years that if a woman wasn't comfortable with a situation, then labour just didn't progress. To digress for a moment, I'd had one such VBAC booked for a home birth where in the middle of her labour, she suddenly piped up,
"Lynn, I need to go to hospital...". No reason - I thought labour had been going well, but she was so sure. We just upped and went. The birth was fine - however, she had a huge bleed just before the placenta birthed. It would've been a blue-light emergency had we'd remained at home, but in hospital, I felt able to relax and observe to see if it settled (and it did) - no emergency initiated. Something told this woman she needed to be in hospital.

So, when after the appointment with the consultant obstetrician, Karen said, *I still want a home birth,* I trusted her intuition on this. The consultant wasn't quite so unwary. Before I left the hospital that day, she gave me a full compliment of IV fluids and lines for my home birth bag, *should a catastrophic rupture of the uterus occur in labour...* Very generous and supportive - but it felt a little chilling.

Whilst I worked alone in the main, even with 'straightforward' VBACs, I always had a back-up midwife available, but in this case, second IM agreed to attend with me - it was a higher risk circumstance. Karen had a lovely problem free pregnancy and spontaneous labour at term, no other challenges. Well, she didn't, but I did. I arrived at her house, established soon after (visually rather than with VE, as my usual practice) that she was in well-established labour and called my back up to attend. No answer. I tried another couple of times, only ever getting an answer-phone message. Was she at another labour? Surely not - her next client wasn't due for a month or so. After an hour or so of surreptitiously calling my colleague's mobile, I moved on to the home phone. I got the same response - no response. I was at a loss, it was the middle of the night. I was on my own. I discounted trying to get another IM for back-up, as Karen had only accepted my second because they'd met. I reasoned that if I insisted on another practitioner now, I would be giving off a vibe of insecurity or worse, fear - the biggest enemy of birth. No. My mind was made up. But from a professional standpoint, I did decide to call the local SOM on call, to inform her that I was on my own in this high-risk situation. I'm not sure it was helpful, she simply wished me *good luck...*

It's fair to say that I was extremely vigilant during this labour and birth. Karen's pulse remained steady throughout as did the FH. In the end it was a fabulous anti-climax of ordinariness - baby popping out on the bathroom floor, with the placenta following during baby's first feed soon afterwards. All was well that ended well... but I think I had a few more grey hairs...

Midwife Voice

G - A midwife who is no longer practicing - *'I was a former nurse, then a midwife, and I left because I was pressurised into conforming, and I've never been a conformer. Right from being a child, I've always been the one to question. Don't tell me what to do, tell me why you need me to do that, so... it's been in every aspect.'*

Coven contributor - What does it mean to you, to be radical?

My work has always been about knowledge. I've always been curious about what we know, how we know it, and how we can use knowledge to be with women on their journeys. To give people information which will help them decide what's right for them. So my answer is inevitably grounded in that perspective. For me, being radical is quite literally about going to the roots of what we know in order to truly be "with woman." I began to see that this was important when I learned as a young medical and midwifery student about how patriarchal structures have oppressed, erased and hidden women's voices, stories, experiences and knowledge. I also began to see that some of the things we were doing weren't based on good evidence. Sometimes there was no evidence, sometimes there was evidence that we were wilfully taking the wrong approach and I began to see that there were some really deep issues that were creating and maintaining this problem.

Ever since, I have been at work unpacking, questioning, evaluating, speaking out and writing about the knowledge upon which modern maternity care is based. Sometimes that's just with the one woman and family who I'm with in that moment, and who need to know if the evidence really does support the recommendation, and sometimes that's on a global stage. But both are just as important, and they're both about the same thing: going to the roots of what we think we know and asking important questions about whether that knowledge is valid, and whether it serves women and families. And offering good information (which might sometimes contradict the mainstream view, or the NICE guidelines) to those who need to make decisions about their own journey.

There are many things that affect us today that we can better understand by following them to their roots. There are metaphorical knowledge pathways that remain unexplored because they are not profitable, or do not benefit the group or person seeking knowledge. Notions like insurance and risk – which both have a massive impact upon modern maternity care – are rooted in capitalism, fear, slavery and sexism. We have population-level interventions that will only benefit a tiny number of those who are exposed to them but no appetite to seek a more individualised (and often cheaper) approach which might help us identify the people who really need a particular drug or treatment. There is an abundance of evidence that midwifery-led care is better for women and babies but, as this approach doesn't serve those who currently hold power, it is not prioritised. A radical approach to knowledge and to midwifery means that we can dig into these issues and be able to see and explain what is really going on, and that is the start of change.

Some of the things that we can do as a result of what we have learned through history are marvellous, and I'm not suggesting we throw them out. But a lot of what we do in modern maternity care isn't sound, or based on good knowledge. As many analysts have shown, priority is given to the technologies, services and products that serve those who hold power. Many of these technologies have been shown to be ineffective and harmful, and yet the power structures that underpin modern systems of maternity care sometimes mean we have zero evidence (and, often, regard) for things that have served women and families well for millennia. It's important that we enable others to understand how the patriarchy has sought (and still seeks) to oppress and erase women's bodies and voices, in multiple ways. And that alternative approaches are available and possible.

Being radical means, for me, trying to get to the root of these issues in order to understand them, help others to understand them and then, hopefully, be able to take some sort of action to change them. Which does then bring us to the other definition of the word 'radical', which is about departing from what's usual and challenging the status quo. And yes, I guess I can also identify with that element of the notion of being radical, but that's from necessity rather than desire. I don't challenge and campaign for the sake of it. I challenge and campaign because there exists a significant and unjust gap. On the one hand, there are the tenets and ideologies on which modern maternity care is based: risk, distrust, management of women's bodies, the business model and the prioritisation of technology. On the other, midwives have - and are further developing - a body of knowledge which comes from a more thoughtful, woman-centred, physiology-focused perspective, which I would argue better serves serve women and families, including when measured by the standards of the medical model. Those who take such an approach don't deny technologies; they use them as tools within a midwifery model. Those who take a midwifery model approach don't claim that they know everything; they acknowledge that there is much that we don't know. So what does it mean to me to be radical? It means to dig down into the roots of what we know; to question; to unpack and to seek the kind of wisdom that enables us to offer woman-centred midwifery.

Sara Wickham

Sources of Knowledge

Like most people, I access many sources for information when wishing to educate myself about a subject. When it came to midwifery, I already held some strong views considering my philosophy of birth as I had given birth myself three times prior to training. That said, I do not believe that you need to give birth to be a midwife, or that certain experiences imbue you with 'special' knowledge or advantage - I simply acknowledge that my birth history is an influence on what I believe.

One unusual reference I have mined for my basic doctrine of midwifery came from Star Trek. I even shared these principles in Issue 75 of Midwifery Matters in 1997 to round off an article I'd written about attending a home birth as a student midwife (Achieving a Home Birth - Lynn Walcott). The article is fully referenced as I was still firmly in academic mode, keen to demonstrate credibility, but the apparently 'tongue in cheek' doctrine *All I needed to know about midwifery I learned from Star Trek* was a subverted dig at the shortcomings as I saw them, of the training I'd received. Today, I would still stand by this basic list as a creed to practice by.

Article

All I needed to know about midwifery I learned form Star Trek

Non-interference is the prime directive
Humans are highly illogical
Infinite diversity in infinite combinations
Insufficient data does not compute
Seek out new life
When logic fails, trust a hunch
Boldly go where no *midwife* has gone before
Live long and prosper

Lynn Walcott
Midwifery Matters 75 – Winter 1997

I'm still a Star Trek fan, and the following short story was a more recent allusion to the cult TV series.

Article

Future Birth
Inspired by Star Trek and the NHS

Carly was now sure that she was having contractions regularly and that they were getting stronger and longer and closer together, so she woke her partner, Jay. This was the point that they could be admitted to the maternity unit according to the App on her phone. All they had to do was check in on-line. Jay was up immediately and offered to do this whilst Carly got herself sorted. The 'Personalise your Birth' App connected to their local hospital was very straightforward and they'd enjoyed putting together their unique birth plan just last week. All Jay had to do now was press the 'yes' next to the 'in labour?' option and their personally picked midwife would be waiting for them on arrival at the unit.

It was their first baby and after reading everything they could, and speaking to other couples on-line, they knew exactly what kind of midwife they needed: young like them, so that they could relate to her; confident, giving reassurance frequently, and experienced enough to know exactly what would be right for Carly when it came to help with decision-making. They'd submitted the questionnaire and the hospital would be able to select the best match for their needs based on their answers.

They were soon at the reception of the hospital and the App gave them the code to open the door. It was 03:00 and they didn't expect to see many people around, but there were distant headlights in the car park as someone else parked. The Welcome Screen in the foyer lit up as the couple entered, displaying the words:
"Good morning, Carly & Jay, and welcome to Future Birth, the new state-of-the-art hospital supporting women in one-to-one care with their own specially matched midwife."

They smiled at each other. This was so exciting. The futuristic building was only months old and as soon as they toured it last month, they'd been looking forward to this day. The screen changed and they were instructed to follow the violet-coloured lights to their birth suite. They looked down, and as they did so, a gentle purplish glow began to illuminate the floor. They immediately began to follow, and it disappeared behind them but grew brighter in front. After a most enchanting walk of some 10 minutes, following the fairy-tale lights, they reached a purple door with a screen to the left which said:
"Do not enter unless the alarm is sounding." They looked at each other again, but this time quizzically. They'd chosen their wording for the birth room as part of the questionnaire in the birth plan - and it was supposed to say:
"Do not enter - new soul about to be born." Perhaps it would be on another doorway?

Carly's phone vibrated, and just like magic, the door opened. Rock music filled their ears. They'd been expecting Jay's choice of classical and calming music, so this came as a surprise, but just as they stepped in, the door closed automatically behind them, and a figure stepped out of a side room.

"Mornin' Carly, mornin' Jay. Let's get dis show on the road. You don't need me to tell you what's comin', you know what you gotta do. Off we go. You can call me Angie." The grandmotherly midwife with just a hint of a West Indian accent turned on her heels and sauntered away waving her hand for them to follow. They followed, and Carly shrugged her shoulders to Jay's questioning look. Where was the young cool midwife they'd requested? Was this her assistant?

Meanwhile, another couple arrived at the reception. This labouring woman was irritated and telling her partner to hurry up otherwise the baby was going to be born in the doorway. He tried desperately to find the code to get in but the App wasn't cooperating. The woman was about to take the phone off of him and try for herself when he found it and opened the door. The Welcome screen lit up just as the woman had a huge contraction, grabbing hold of her man. Once it subsided, they looked at the screen and it told them to follow the red lights to their birth suite.

They walked fast, the lights anticipating their speed, and within 5 minutes they reached a red door. Another strong contraction took all their attention. The phone vibrated just as the contraction came to an end and the door opened. This baby wasn't going to be long, Carly could tell, and just wanted to get to the birth room, strip off, and get on with it, probably on all fours on the floor like last time. They stepped in. Where was the midwife? Carly could feel another contraction coming and grabbed Jay as it intensified.

"Hello, Carly and Jay......oh this looks promising. I'm your midwife, Jessica. Oh that's right breathe through it. Well done Jay, you must've been to classes. I can see you know how to support your partner, anyone would think you'd done this before! That's it, nearly over, and then perhaps you'd like to have a bit of a soak in the beautiful birth pool, it's all ready for you."

Carly came out of her contraction, looked at the smiling young face, and then in confusion at Jay. And was that classical music she could hear?

"I thought we agreed on Muse, what's this rubbish?" Carly glared at Jay, then, looking at the midwife asked, "Birth pool? I didn't request that. Last time it happened so quick that I ... oh no".

She broke off as another contraction seized her and she grabbed hold of the midwife's arm to steady herself.

"That's it Carly......oh, that's a strong one. You're squeezing really quite hard, let's get to the birth room before another one comes. There you go, it's almost over. Aren't you good at this ...you may need something more than water ... what did you mean last time? I'll just go and check your notes." And Jessica was gone.

Carly was immediately taken over by another contraction and groaned loudly and deeply as she dropped to the floor onto her hands and knees.

Meanwhile, the other Carly and Jay followed midwife Angie into the birth room and looked around. Where was the pool?

"Is there another room with the pool?" Jay tried to shout over the loud soundtrack. Angie seemed oblivious to them, singing along as she sorted things onto a trolley and stared at a screen on the wall that was headed, 'Birth Plan - Carly and Jay'. Jay was about to repeat the question when Carly cried out, "Jay, quick, I can feel a tightening coming at last."

Jay supported Carly, trying to soothe her but was increasingly irritated by Muse's 'Newborn' bellowing out into the room. As Carly recovered, seconds later, Angie looked at them both, hand on hip. "Is that it?" she asked. "I think you're gonna have a longer labour dis time."

"This time?" they chorused. Angie then stared, and seemed to be looking at them properly for the first time.

Back in the red suite, Jay had joined Carly on the floor just in time to catch the baby emerging from its mother's body.

"I think there's been a ..." and Jessica's voice was interrupted by a loud baby's cry. "Oh!" Jessica appeared. "The notes say that Jay is the biological mother, this doesn't make sense?"

Midwife Angie continued to stare. Carly and Jay stared back. "Is this about the pool?' asked Jay, 'we were told it was guaranteed."

"Pool? I don't know about no pool." Carly glared first at Angie, then Jay. "What the hell?" Carly was angry. "Just dat it says Jay is the biological father", Angie tried to make sense of it all, and then added, "Oh ... I see", and turned to the screen, swiping through a few pages added: "You're the wrong Carly and Jay. I better press the emergency ..." but was unable to finish as a high-pitched alarm sounded and the lights started flashing.

The next day, the CEO of 'Future Birth' held a press conference. "Can I just say, that we are very sorry to have caused any distress and that we are investigating our systems as I speak. Until we sort out the glitches in the programs, this hospital will remain closed to women in labour. However, our holographic midwives will continue to practice in the antenatal and postnatal wards offering the most up to date evidence-based practice in the world, personally tailored to each and every woman."

Lynn R S Genevieve

Midwifery Matters 160 - Spring 2019

Midwife Voice

E - An ARM member who has applied to train as a midwife - *'I'm an aspiring student midwife. So I've finally plucked up the courage this year, to apply, very late in the day. For me, it's the reason I applied – it's because of such poor care I had when I had my wee girl last July. In the run up, it was very much, "but the textbook says, but this says" and to me, being radical is to think, well actually, no! Everybody's different, everybody's unique, and because the text book says this is what should happen, isn't necessarily what is best for that person, and for me, is the way I would practice. From my usual history, at work, I'm not afraid to question things and push boundaries, and things like that. So, when I discovered ARM, I was absolutely overjoyed, because I feel that you guys will be thinking along the same lines as me and hopefully if I get in, I can push that forward as well...'*

Midwife Voice

B - A student member - *'I think for me, being radical means asking why all of the time. Why? I think toddlers are radical because that's all they do all the time 's 'Why? Why? Why?' and I think we forget sometimes to be curious, and to question things, and to test our understanding, and being radical to me means to ask why...'*

When it comes to evidence informed practice, I have always held a particular point of view. Essentially based on individual care, I still feel that my experiences are valid for midwives today and readily share my opinions. I commented on a controversial area of practice in Midwifery Matters in 2020.

Article

Comment re: OASI 'Care' Bundle: First Do No Harm

Whilst I am retired from midwifery I have heard much about the OASI Care Bundle that Margaret Jowitt wrote about in the Spring issue of MM. As six pages were devoted to this analysis I think that it is fair to say it's an important and emotive subject. Meeting up with my cohort of midwife trainees a yearly event, at the end of last year was also dominated by talk of this intervention. We qualified more than twenty years ago and these five practising midwives were all agreed that this 'care' bundle was controversial at best, but ultimately their group opinion was that it was harmful.

The conversations recounted, reminded me of the late Mary Cronk's stories of *doing good by stealth* which Margaret alluded to in her article:

"Imposing this care bundle risks a return to the old days when episiotomies could be cut after the birth (yes rarely, but it happened) to prevent disciplinary action. (Mary Cronk used to drop the scissors instead...)"

My cohort was trained 1994-97 in Berkshire and we were very much a part of the HOOP trial (Sleep 1998) that Margaret cites as one of the few studies that have tested elements of the OASI bundle. I remember well recruiting women in the community for the trial and later the excitement as a student working on labour ward when a woman in labour arrived and I would be given the job of nipping out to quickly pick up a sealed gold envelope (I'm sure it was gold...) before the baby's head crowned, which contained the instructions *'Hands On' Or 'Poised'.* It was an illuminating time to train as some mentors would be visibly pleased to be able to *"just let the woman and nature birth her baby"* Hands Poised, whilst others twitched with the Hands Poised instruction, often resorting to some element of using a Hands On technique as *"the trial guideline still left it up to the individual midwife to decide if it was needed..."* - it often was... apparently.

I therefore learnt as a student midwife early on, two things: the first, babies can actually be born without the midwife using her hands (who knew?) and the second, midwives sometimes lie. Throughout my career both these assertions were reinforced time and time again.

It's uncomfortable, isn't it? Admitting this truth, that our profession is vulnerable to this human failing of telling lies. It works both ways, positively, as in *doing good by stealth* as well as negatively, for example when a community midwife accused me of assaulting a student midwife; I had just ejected her and the student from the house, verbally... she was aggrieved - I'd complained to the Supervisor of Midwives. (The ensuing complaint lasted a year, and has been brought to my mind recently whilst writing my memoir). I have seen - on paper and in person - and heard midwives lie in cases before the NMC and I have witnessed these serious transgressions numerous times in clinical situations - it has always riled me. Midwives lie... Doctors lie... nurses lie... people lie... I'm sorry but it is a fact, one that the professions seem reluctant to address. But that's a whole other article...

Getting back to Margaret's excellent article and HOOP, she suggests *"observing the practice of midwives with particularly low rates"* of anal sphincter injury. By simply adopting what the midwives did in the USA years ago when midwifery was making a comeback and MANA needed to 'prove' that midwives are 'safe' - individual audits. Why could this not be part of a midwife's CPD?

I know from working in an NHS stand alone midwifery unit that auditing outcomes is very revealing. I recall one year the audit of our small group of midwives revealed that one particular midwife sutured much more often, the result of having a belief that to repair an episiotomy was better than the possibility of a large tear; *an episiotomy just in case* meant that many women inevitably ended up with perineal damage that may not have required suturing or perhaps, were deprived of an intact perineum. In her defence, almost certainly she was trained at the time Margaret mentions in her article, when *"...it was thought that episiotomy was essential for all women."*

Later working as an Independent Midwife and part of the IMA, I was pleased to record outcomes and was reassured by figures that supported a *Hands Poised* approach from the point of view of perineal damage; I never had a third degree tear and suturing was minimal. I'm pretty sure that IM's today would be able to attest to similar. As Margaret reports a midwife in Australia asserting: *"We need to take responsibility for our own practice and stop colluding in disrespectful maternity care."*

Midwifery has never been an easy profession, and my heart goes out to all medical practitioners at this difficult time. Covid-19 has added an extra dimension to *'good practice'* as if the pressures within the NHS weren't enough! My musings on this strange time of lockdown have as usual, alluded to my regular habit of bringing everything in life back to birth - once a midwife always a midwife. So it is, that I have looked at the *guidance* for social distancing from a personal point of view, much like I used to weigh up the risks for women birthing at home against medical advice or local guidelines.

I was out on a long walk, I do this once a week in lieu of a walk with the local walking group and I was in a comparatively remote area for several hours. I didn't see a soul. I was musing on my friends and family in the South of England and how they were trying their best to keep their social distance whilst out getting 'exercise', is it an hour a day that has been suggested? They tell me it's like Piccadilly Circus most days as everyone has time to do this now. Here I was, wandering the tracks in the hills, some miles from home, completely at peace enjoying my day - should I feel guilty for being out for so long? My fellow group walkers are all staying very close to home - no hill walks, no longer than an hour. I started comparing my attitude to the 'daily exercise' with the way I worked as a midwife. It's all just guidelines, I thought - just there as what is best for a population - just like guidelines in clinical practice. I'd weighed up my choices, I could adhere to the guideline, spend an hour close to home wandering the same well worn track or roadside, or I could be out here, enjoying an ancient right of way miles from anywhere. My fellow walkers were taking the 'advice' from the mountain rescue teams to the letter; what if we injure ourselves and need to be airlifted out? That's valuable medical team's time... what if? Most of them have been walking these hills twenty years or more without incident. But what if?

I'd weighed up my own risks, I'm not as old as most of the group, many of whom have chronic conditions that require medication. I do not walk in the challenging mountain ranges, and keep to well known pathways. My husband can track me on my phone... Just like when weighing up a home birth and the individual risks to a mother, I mused. Over fifty percent of my clients when I was an independent midwife were deemed as high risk and shouldn't have a home birth... according to the guidelines. But we'd weighed up their individual risks and planned well, it was rarely a problem; my transfer rate was far less than the community midwives at the local midwifery led unit. This is it, I thought, each of us has to weigh up the risks we are presented with and make decisions for ourselves.

This may not be the easiest time to be *with woman* and strong and I am well aware that suggesting midwives resist an obstetric edict that is not proven as best practice from the comfort of my home as a retiree I may come across as having no idea what it's like out there. But I will never forget and the biggest gift of menopause for me has been learning to live true to myself. But it doesn't stop me feeling guilty about enjoying lockdown...

Lynn R S Genevieve
Midwifery Matters 165 - June 2020

Midwife Voice
F - Midwife - '*...questioning everything and wanting to be able to step outside and not be just a pawn in the system, and actually putting the woman or birthing person at the centre of their decision-making and respecting them for it. I don't think that's that radical really. I question even the fact that what I feel and believe, is radical at all? Because it seems to be the most normal thing ever, for me to want to work in a way that listens to women, and to search. For me it's always being about searching out the breadth of midwifery and birth practice. That we're sold a story, it's a small box and yet the truth is so much bigger than that, and it feels like yes, radical to me...was searching through the Internet when 20 years ago, when you had to go into so many pages and stories to find out more truth, about how birth works and how women give birth in such diverse situations...*'

A Birth Story

How about a VBA4Cs? There's a rare test. In this case, the woman had tried after her first LSCS to have a VBAC with every labour - supported by the hospital... as long as she agreed to labour *in* the hospital. Ginny had deduced that this was the problem - the real reason why she could not give birth vaginally. She trusted her body, knew that she was capable - had kept trying, but come to the conclusion (and I couldn't disagree with her logic) that the only thing stopping her was the environment - more specifically, the people 'supporting' her; they did not share her confidence. Her solution? To hire IMs to attend her at home. The final decision to book with me had been made after a Consultant obstetrician appointment where the doctor declared,

"...if you insist on going ahead with labour after four caesareans, you're not labouring here...". Nice man! As I explained to Ginny, he was in cloud cuckoo land if he thought that he had the right to deny her access to the NHS hospital. Outrageous.

Together with my back up, we visited Ginny often, winning over the sceptic family (husband and Ginny's mother) who had been frightened by the Consultant's outburst. By the time Ginny spontaneously laboured at term, they were all in situ and supportive as Ginny laboured in her birth pool... and after only six hours, had a lovely, uneventful water birth. Again... women know what they know. I have always trusted that women will never knowingly put their babies at risk. Over and over again, my trust was upheld during my career as a midwife.

Coven Contribution

What does it mean to be radical? A lament.

I have procrastinated over answering this question, going right up to the deadline and beyond, procrastination which does not reflect the sense of honour I feel to have been asked for my contribution to this collection of Midwives' Voices by Lynn Genevieve, an inspiring radical midwife[1] herself. My prevarication is because after more than twenty-four proud years as a member of the Association of Radical Midwives (ARM), I am no longer sure what it means to be radical, or even what it means to be a midwife. In addition to my uncertainty about what it means to be radical, I am hesitating over renewing my midwifery registration and even of retaining my precious ARM membership.

I have finally taken Lynn's question as an opportunity for a somewhat meandering exploration of being radical and being a midwife – for me the two go together somehow. The whole discussion is, at least partly, a lament for a way of being a midwife that is starting to feel impossible for me. I hope my reflections resonate with some of the readers of this collection, and help to form this living archive of voices to assist future generations to understand what it is like to be a midwife in England in 2021. As I am a storyteller as well as a midwife (I am currently writing a memoir), I will begin with a story and let the exploration flow out from there.

The only radical midwife in the room

One afternoon about ten years ago, I was in a stuffy room in the suite of research offices of our local hospital. The room was crowded with midwives and obstetricians sitting in rows. Standing at the opposite end of the room to me was Professor Jim Thornton, one of the leading researchers of a study that we were all working on into induction of labour for women over the age of thirty-five (the 35/39 Trial, reported in Walker, 2016). It was an important meeting of all the people who had been involved with that trial and I remember feeling that I was the only one in the room – the picture I have in my mind is of me standing to face him but I may have misremembered this - arguing with Jim about the nuance of how to publish our findings and whether we should recommend induction of labour (IOL).

Our results showed that IOL didn't appear to lead to more caesareans, but we had too little data about any other outcomes to recommend induction of labour for all. I was pretty scared to stand up and argue, but Jim relished the debate, using the phrase 'Grace versus Thornton' and I could not believe that it was down to me to take a stand that was different to that of (what felt like) the entire room and in particular an eminent professor of obstetrics. No doubt there were other discussions, and my contribution was not as decisive as this recollection may imply. My point is less about my actual role, and more to do with that sense of speaking out even when it may be unpopular to do so.

Mary Cronk, who in earlier years had been an independent midwife colleague of mine and an inspiration, always talked about speaking up even if your knees were knocking, and I genuinely felt shaky during this exchange which I imagine Jim would be quite surprised about. But I think this story illustrates that for me being radical is being true to myself and my beliefs (while respecting those of others) even if they are minority beliefs, or seem extreme in that particular setting. To me my beliefs are not extreme of course! They are my beliefs and as such they are experienced by me as simply how I think, what seems evident to me. But because they are sometimes not mainstream beliefs, they may be perceived by others as radical in the sense of the definition of the word 'radical' described by the Cambridge Dictionary meaning, "believing or expressing the belief that there should be great or extreme social or political change". To be worried about universal induction of labour does not seem extreme to me; the extreme position as far as I see it is to interfere with birth physiology with little thought for any consequences bar getting the baby out as quickly as possible. Yet that kind of thinking (to promote induction of labour) is somehow not seen as radical but as sensible and safety-conscious; it is fast becoming the mainstream position.

Of course, there are no doubt people who would say it is not a particularly radical thing for a midwife to be involved in a research trial into induction of labour in the first place. Indeed, that was exactly what I wondered when I was asked to be the midwife representative on the Trial Steering Committee. But the trial would have gone ahead with or without me, and I had been impressed by the team's dedication to the aim of reducing stillbirth, an aim I share. And I felt that at least I could represent a midwifery – possibly a radical midwifery – view that would otherwise be absent.

Midwives and the 'swan effect'

That story is one small example of the kind of position that many 'radical' midwives find ourselves in, though perhaps more usually in the clinical rather than the research setting. I have always had a clinical caseload even while carrying out research, and was one of the small number of midwives in the UK who worked as an independent midwife (IM), living my radical values by supporting women who made their own choices in childbirth. However, we independent midwives lost all forms of indemnity that allowed us to serve women in this way, at least partly because of the actions of the Royal College of Midwives (RCM) and Nursing and Midwifery Council (NMC).

This means that the existing maternity services (run by the NHS and small private providers) are now the only legal way in which midwives can support women in childbirth, but we experience parts of the services as troubling from an ethical perspective. We participate because we want to fulfil our midwifery calling by caring for women and we tend to think we can make a difference by being as radical as we can be under the circumstances.

Mandi Scamell reports on an ethnographic study of midwives' talk and practice in which the "swan effect" was identified, meaning that midwives present a serene, confident appearance but "under the water our little feet are flapping about like mad" overseeing a huge range of monitoring and governance activities (page 987, Scamell, 2011). Scamell contends that "through routine surveillance practices, midwives implicitly introduce uncertainty, amplify risk and thereby disturb and restrict the possibility that women can achieve a normal birth" (page 996, ibid), while we present ourselves and even believe in ourselves as being in favour of women's choices and of freedom. Does this mean we are fooling ourselves if we even think we can be radical within this system? It cannot be easy to be radical when the default setting is to monitor, observe and control women and women's bodies.

I know I'm not alone in feeling that midwives are often directly involved in – feel ourselves colluding with – this system. We apply CTG belts even though we know the evidence doesn't support their routine use. We measure symphysis/fundal height rather than relying on the skill of our own hands, and the knowledge of the woman, to tell us how the baby is growing.

We plot those measurements on personalised growth charts that don't prevent poor outcomes and have a high false positive rate (Thornton, 2019).

We then refer women for ultrasound scans, scans which may have bioeffects on developing cells and tissues and for which few risk/benefit analyses are conducted (see for instance, Abramovitz, 2013). Then, if the scan decides that the baby is too small, or too big, even though we know the measurements are likely to be inaccurate, we refer women for further interventions that may cause more harm than good. In this litigious age if you take action and it all goes pear-shaped, then no one will blame you, whereas if you don't act, if you don't recommend that caesarean, you will be castigated for not saving the baby even though caesareans carry substantial risks of their own.

Why do radical midwives go along with all this? Much of our compliance with these systems is to do with fear of discipline, of punishment by the Nursing and Midwifery Council. However, more subtle and even stronger than this fear is something more akin to institutionalisation. We do things the way everyone else does them, the way we were taught. We tend to lack the autonomy to support clients to make decisions that challenge the orthodox mainstream approach to childbearing even though research evidence supports one-to-one midwifery care and a judicious use of obstetric interventions.

Is there anything radical at all about modern midwifery?

This all sounds incredibly negative, but in spite of the way in which midwives and women are edged into compliance with routine surveillance and interventions, the relationship between mother and midwife, particularly in continuity of carer models, can still contain elements of the radical. Even where continuity models don't exist, the skill of midwives at developing relationships, including within medicalised settings, means that many women are satisfied with their maternity care (Care Quality Commission, 2019).

Earlier, I discussed radicalism as a kind of extremism even

if what is seen as extreme depends on the perspective of the viewer. However, the word 'radical' has its origins in late Middle English and relates to the 'root' of a thing or act (from late Latin *radicalis*). This is the sense in which the word is used by the Association of Radical Midwives and according to this meaning, it is not that an act or belief is outside of the mainstream that makes it radical; being radical means being rooted in the origins of a belief, experience or activity. If you believe, as I do, that being a midwife means being 'with woman', then there are many ways to demonstrate this. Some manage it through their scholarly work in an academic setting; some are brilliant midwifery leaders; and I would argue any midwife who devotedly maintains connection with a woman is being a radical midwife, whether in a high-tech medicalised setting or at a home birth.

I recall a tiny little midwife (I will call her Margaret) I met as a student and who seemed to me the epitome of a non-radical midwife. She was good company in the midwives' sitting room, but I was taken aback by things I saw her do. I was shocked by the way she would rather cut an episiotomy than wait for the perineum to stretch, and I found it bewildering that she loved to put a woman on an electronic fetal monitoring machine, preferably with a nice solid epidural.

Yet Margaret taught me something the day I saw her standing firm while a labouring woman hung from her neck, dripping with sweat. That woman needed a rock of strength and support and Margaret was there to provide that small but indefatigable rock. How many humans would be prepared to do that, to stand there while a large, tall, naked stranger clung to and dripped on them, without a word of complaint? I still remember the genuine smile stretched across Margaret's face when the woman pushed out her baby.

That occasion opened my eyes to the complexity of this issue of who is and who isn't a midwife, let alone who is a radical midwife. I knew then that Margaret had that bit of extra something that makes someone a midwife, even if she had been conditioned to behave in ways I found troubling and that were sometimes harmful. And it might well be that some of the 'midwives' who talk a better talk than Margaret, and don't do some of the questionable things she did, don't have that something. They don't have what it takes to be fully present with a woman; it is a rare gift and it is not only conferred on the hippy midwives among us.

Margaret is a controversial example of a radical midwife and I don't condone or belittle some of her harmful practices. But perhaps even more controversial is the way in which midwives – including you and me - have always found ways to support women that covertly defy the surveillance and control system – in other words, have found ways in which to be radical. Mary Cronk tells of dropping the episiotomy scissors on the floor and how many midwives have diagnosed a 'cervical lip' which they know will buy the woman an hour or two of time before she is on the clock to push out her baby – probably most midwives?

But how radical is it to 'do good by stealth'?

Independent midwifery and autonomy

Fairly early on in my midwifery career, after six years with the NHS, I decided to go independent which certainly felt like the radical choice that would allow me to not only do good by stealth, but openly. I was living the deeper meaning of the word radical, going back to the roots of midwifery, being with woman. For a few golden years, my clients and I were more or less free to take the decisions that were best for them.

The clients had bodily autonomy, while I had clinical autonomy. It felt like freedom, and I attended many home births (and some hospital births) where women birthed in their own power, and I witnessed this. I also occasionally attended births where we had to transfer for a complication, and I sometimes discovered my autonomy (and that of the client) stopped at the hospital door. I don't want to claim I ever achieved midwifery perfection! I am human, I made mistakes. But for the most part it was a good way to work for both me and my clients, rooted in inherent, embodied wisdom and integrity.

However, independent midwives lost our autonomy, arguably when insurance became a legal necessity, a loss that was cruelly rubber-stamped when Statutory Supervision of Midwifery was removed. We have spent the last 8 years fighting a rearguard action to little avail. Independent midwifery in the UK in its previous form – where mothers could make their own decisions during pregnancy and birth and be supported wholeheartedly by midwives – is now extinct. Even where we supposedly support a woman's choice, governance procedures and the lack of the Supervisor of Midwives for both NHS and non-NHS midwives often means taking a risk-based rather than a woman-centred approach.

We are like the midwives in Mandie Scamell's article – saying we support women's choices, even believing it ourselves, while the risk-based documentation and governance procedures tell a different story. We have to ram home the supposed 'risks' of anything that is outside of 'guidelines' which are now more accurately described as 'policies' than clinical guidelines. Having to reiterate to women the risks of actions which go against guidelines, while not being allowed to talk about the risks of inductions, of scans, of measurements, of surveillance itself, makes it much harder to act as a radical midwife, though obviously in spite of this some midwives do still raise their heads above the parapet. These exceptional midwives continue to speak up, often the lone voice in the room, and they do sometimes have great triumphs.

Such triumphs include putting into practice the aims of the Better Births maternity transformation programme, and setting up home birth or continuity teams that may help obviate the overall controlling and coercive mainstream maternity environment. Some organisations could even be described as radical, with management that supports these initiatives in spite of lack of resources and with never enough staff.

Being radical means having courage

Being radical is about being true to my roots and living with integrity. I must dig deep into myself to find the courage to not be part of the crowd if the crowd does not share my values. I must find the courage to stand up for my rights, and the rights of others. I think it is possible to be a radical midwife and still be registered, but it is not easy. I believe in virtually every word of the NMC Code, but it is increasingly difficult to support women to make their own choices wholeheartedly without battle or subterfuge.

I don't know if I even want to go to births anymore – I have been doing it for a long time now and feel weary.

I considered following in the footsteps of Lynn Genevieve herself, whose most famous article of the dozens she has written for Midwifery Matters was 'Wasn't I Just Made For This Life?' (Walcott, 2009). That article by Lynn presages my lament; she left clinical midwifery during what to me was still a golden time, but she saw the writing on the wall very clearly. On re-reading, twelve years after she wrote it, that article stills feels radical. Women should not have to wade through pages of research evidence before they make decisions about themselves and their bodies? Heresy!

When my registration came up for renewal, I did not immediately apply for revalidation. But six months on I applied for and gained readmission to the NMC register. A friend said to me, 'you earned your registration'. I did earn it, and I will try to live up to the ideals of the Code, even when that is made difficult – sometimes by the NMC itself.

Radical community

I started this discussion with the idea that to be radical, for me, is to act with integrity to my own beliefs, even if those beliefs are not held by others around me. However, while I might have been the only radical midwife in a room on many occasions during my midwifery career of 24 years, my backbone was stiffened by all the other feminist radical midwives of the ARM. For all those years of standing out and speaking up, I had the support, love and validation that we all, as social beings, need.

The Association of Radical Midwives was "formed in 1976 by a small group of student midwives from different training schools who were alarmed by the apparent trend towards maternity nurse status in their training". Many times over the years, we gathered together in rooms and were no longer the only one. We were together. The knitting would come out, some of us would sip tea and others wine, while we told stories, endless stories, celebrating each other when we stood up for our women and holding space for the broken ones, allowing them to grieve and weep when overcome by setback or tragedy, so they could dry their tears and step out once more. It was a sisterhood.

I not only lament the state of radical midwifery in general but the way in which ARM is also changing. It no longer feels to me like a place where my stories will always be welcome. Instead, I am on my guard, defending myself and arguing for the very principles on which the ARM constitution was founded.

A new kind of activism has hit various midwifery, birth and breastfeeding organisations, including ARM. A small number of activists want to change our philosophy and our language in the name of inclusion, to use phrases such as 'birthing people' in addition to or instead of 'women' for those who can give birth. This might seem a relatively small thing; who doesn't want to be inclusive? I certainly do, and it should go without saying that I believe that all, including those who identify as trans and non-binary, are entitled to the best possible health care in every setting including maternity.

But language really matters, and the change of language reflects an underpinning ideology of gender with which I do not agree. I believe it plays into the hands of patriarchy if birth is seen as anything other than a women's issue. How can you organise as an oppressed group if you can't name yourself? Would you ask a group of working class people to add, 'and other people' to their self-description? It makes a mockery of it! We are all people, of course we are, but we need to be able to name ourselves as a sex-class in order to combat our oppression.

It is impossible to encapsulate my entire Marxist-feminist political philosophy in a paragraph or two, but in simplistic terms, I believe sex is not a malleable social construct, nor is sex a spectrum. Biological sex is a material reality and binary. People with disorders of sexual development ('intersex') should not be used to bolster arguments for sex as a spectrum.

Birth is a women's issue. Control and repression of female people is particularly apparent where childbirth is concerned, when the female body is at its most powerful, and therefore the racist patriarchal capitalist state needs to exert maximum control within maternity systems. We see this at every level of such systems, and experience this control as individual, embodied beings.

As the women's liberation movement asserts, the personal is political. For me it is therefore of vital political importance that we retain the legitimacy to speak of childbirth as a women's issue. I do know trans people who share similar ideas and who support women's right to self-determination as well as fighting for the rights of trans people. I am against discrimination.

ARM is known as a feminist organisation and that has always meant a range of views. All involved with birth are welcome be part of ARM however they identify. However, I have been accused of 'hate crime' and wanting poor outcomes for trans people, accusations I find painful, especially within what was my main midwifery circle of mutual support.

I am a working class woman and have spent my whole adult life campaigning - with the miners and other working class people fighting for wages and jobs; against apartheid and against racism; standing up to defy Clause 28; against the corporations and states who cause climate change; for the right to abortion and bodily autonomy in childbirth. My midwifery is one way in which I lived and expressed my radical values, inspired by midwives such as Mavis Kirkham who was one of the founders of the Association of Radical Midwives and by all the other brilliant midwives and birth activists who have made ARM such a force for good. I hope I contributed to ARM during the time I led on the total rebrand of the organisation and the two years I was editor of our beloved journal, Midwifery Matters.

I have faith that we ARM sisters will eventually forgive each other for these recent hurts. We have too much in common to allow this issue to divide us for long. In the meantime, I have pulled back from involvement with ARM and sought companionship in other spaces, including parts of the 'gender critical' community. I am concentrating on my PhD in creative writing, finishing my memoir entitled 'With Woman'.

I am still radical and getting more radical, unable to keep my mouth shut even if my legs shake when I speak. My roots hold me firm in spite of the trembling. But I can live with myself and I have my integrity. That is what it means to me to be radical.

References

Abramowicz JS. Benefits and risks of ultrasound in pregnancy. Semin Perinatol. 2013 Oct;37(5):295-300. https://pubmed.ncbi.nlm.nih.gov/24176149/

Care Quality Commission (2019) Maternity Services Survey 2019. CQC.

Hayton, Debbie (2021). Caitlin Jenner is right about transgender athletes and women's sports. The Spectator, 3rd May 2021 https://www.spectator.co.uk/article/caitlyn-jenner-is-right-about-transgender-athletes-and-women-s-sports

Scamell, M. (2011). The swan effect in midwifery talk and practice: a tension between normality and the language of risk. Sociology of Health and Illness, 33(7), pp. 987- 1001. doi: 10.1111/j.1467-9566.2011.01366.x

Thornton, Jim (2019) Fetal Growth Charts in Ripe Tomato Blog. https://ripe-tomato.org/fetal-growth-charts/

Walcott, Lynn (2009) Wasn't I Just Made For This Life? Midwifery Matters, 23 pp 10 – 12

Walker, Kate et al (2016) Randomized Trial of Labor Induction in Women 35 Years of Age or Older.
New England Journal of Medicine 2016; 374:813-822

Nicky Grace
Midwyfe

Article

Story Telling and its Influence in Passing Birth Culture through the Generations

Nessa McHugh
Senior lecturer in midwifery, De Montfort University, Leicester

Birth is not only a universal biological event, but also a culturally patterned process. Various rituals and symbols mark the transition from one phase of life to another for both mother and child. These birth practices are based on certain conceptions about the body and reflect values and themes of the culture. (Cominsky 1982)

THE PHYSIOLOGY OF BIRTH remains constant across all cultures, however birth is more than just a physiological event. The sociocultural context of birth will deeply influence the meanings and interpretations we make about the experience of birth. Each birth that a woman experiences, whether it is her first or her fifth is a new and unique experience. Women do not enter into any pregnancy or birth without prior information; they will already have preconceptions about what their birth experience may be like. They will have had mothers, friends, sisters and aunts to tell them the stories of their births. It is from this information that women imbibe the cultural context which will define their birth experience.

Story telling is a powerful cultural medium, but not one that is commonly recognised as a valid source of knowledge in the contemporary environment of scientific knowledge, where professional groups appear to be almost in competition with each other to offer the definitive version of authoritative knowledge. Marshall (1993) states quite clearly that expert advice from both doctors and psychologists concerning pregnancy and motherhood, which is based upon observation rather than experience, is perceived as more valid than women's experiences.

Storytelling relies on the oral transmission of information, it is not a fixed source and its content shifts subtly over time and, the more the tale is told. Story telling is not scientific and exact; as such, it is not considered as a source of valid knowledge and indeed may be frowned upon by more formal providers of knowledge.

At present there are so many gaps in the average woman's knowledge of pregnancy that she is extremely vulnerable to the many old wives tales, horror stories and unfounded advice that continues to surround motherhood, and there is no comprehensive work to which she can turn to relieve her anxieties and answer her questions. (Bourne, 1979)

Many women's magazines are full of real-life stories. readers' experiences which are there to be shared and discussed. Such stories serve to reinforce cultural norms, a sense of what is real, what is perceived as negative. and what is perceived as positive. It would seem given the variety of such publications that they are both popular and profitable. Here the worlds of the formal and lay knowledge merge. An analysis of pregnancy publications (McHugh, 1993) would suggest that populist formats are used to reinforce professional and therefore dominant birth agendas. It could therefore be argued that the cultural understanding of birth has been manipulated into a new techno-medical context.

The contextual understanding of birth is crucial to how we negotiate the birth experience as one of life's major rites of passage. Van Gennep (1909) defined a rite of passage as a series of rituals designed to lead us from one social status to another.

Van Gennep's Rites of Passage:

Separation

The woman is gradually separated from society and her family group. Professionals act as gatekeepers to knowledge. Rituals relating to health practices and dietary requirements are adhered to. Antenatal care is a highly ritualised process.

Liminality

This is where the woman is between roles.

Labour is a liminal experience. Transitional rites often involve pain and keepers of knowledge who steer the individuals through the transformational process.

Re-incorporation

This stage is intended to re-integrate the woman back into the social group and establish her new position in society as a mother.

The movement from one social role to another is a time of potential vulnerability, where clearly understood roles no longer exist, as we understand them. Culturally we deal with this danger by producing a set of internally consistent and mutually dependent practices, which makes sense in a given cultural setting. This could then imply that whatever system is employed for childbirth will be culturally perceived to be the best by those involved with it.

The idea of maintaining the cohesiveness of a society through the consistency of roles passed on through the generations can shed light on the importance of birth stories and what exactly we understand about our own cultures of birth.

For many women being a mother as well as having a woman as a mother provides a profound experience of human connection. The adult experiences as well as childhood experiences, contribute to the evolution of a sense of connection which is consistent with our observations, that connectedness with others is one of the most complicated human achievements requiring a high level of development. (Belenky et al, 1997)

The valuing of the experience of human connection is one of the points that separates out Cartesian definitions of knowledge, and arguably therefore the dominant knowledge frameworks from the sense of interconnectedness which arises from birth and the subculture of women's knowledge. Fox Keller (1985) has suggested that the process of Cartesian duality which underpins much of contemporary scientific/medical belief represents a masculine epistemological stance. Here the focus is on detachment; detachment from emotions, personal interests, but primarily from the object itself.

The scientific mind is set apart from what is to be known, that is, from nature, and its autonomy is guaranteed. By setting apart its modes of knowing from those in which that dichotomy is threatened. In this process, the masculine characterisation of both the scientific and its modes of access to knowledge is significant.
(Fox-Keller, 1985)

Birth is a prime source of culturally shared experience, but what happens when the knowledge of interconnection is subsumed by a dominant cultural force? It is possible to propose three possible outcomes when an essentially antagonistic and dominant cultural force dictates which knowledge is valid and which can be dismissed. When a birth story is passed on, the telling of the experience is part of the normalising process.

The way the story will be told will place a value judgement on the events that occurred. So, for example, an ability to deal with the experience will be transmitted as a positive or negative part of the overall experience. In Britain the vast majority of women expect to give birth in a hospital. This has become part of our process of normalisation. Epidurals are frequently seen as a normal part of childbirth and it can be argued that the accompanying morbidity risks of epidurals are not always discussed fully with women before consent. Pain is often considered to be overwhelming without pharmaceutical analgesia and therefore birth without some form of analgesic is feared and seen as unacceptable. Induction of labour for social reasons still occurs in British hospitals, despite the potential problems that may be associated with an induced labour.

I was born on August 19th 1979 in Wythenshawe Hospital. Mum was induced so Grandad could go over to Ireland. Mum said the 'nurses' looked after me in the nursery so she could rest. (Extract from a 20 year old woman's personal birth story).

The above quotation is part of a number of birth stories collected together to explore how knowledge is transmitted and transmuted. Here the young woman readily accepted that hospital birth was normal (normality here being culturally not physiologically defined). Induction of labour for social reasons was not perceived by either the mother or the daughter to be problematic and the expectation was that nurses looked after babies. The knowledge here is of an event that occurred twenty years ago but for this young woman this becomes part of her perceptions of birth, and ties in with what she would anticipate for herself. Further discussion revealed a fear of pain and the perception that epidurals were the best way to make the 'ordeal' bearable.

Using this birth story it is possible to see how the dominant birth beliefs can dominate two generations of women ensuring that birth is controlled, and beliefs are linked into to the paternalistic 'they know best' thought pattern. The current health systems would appear to foster the expectation that women should relinquish their will and rights, becoming subjugated to a technocratic system of birth with no right to control over their own bodies and experiences.

The second strand involved in the structures of birth cultures and beliefs is that of subverting the system. Here the stories told undermine perceived authority and show how women can be self-determining through subversion.

When asked if my GP had a problem with my baby being born in water at home I replied, 'No '. Of course he didn't have a problem my other friend retorted - you never told him. Why should I? (Extract from a 37 year old woman's birth story).

In the above extract the woman is very aware that she has subverted the usual system. This woman knew what she wanted and was determined to go ahead with it. She was aware that the GP would consider her birth choices to be unacceptable, so had decided against informing him. In this instance the midwives at her birth had no contact with this particular GP and so confrontation was avoided.

This provides an example of the women who are aware of the conventional norms and are able to by-pass both the norms and confrontation. This represents a form of challenge to the system, but it is covert and almost takes the form of a subliminal rebellion. The message to this woman's daughter was that you can subvert dominant birth beliefs and retain control over your own birth and your own body. However although this birth story has many positives there are elements of manipulation as opposed to assertiveness. There is no direct challenge to the dominant birth beliefs and as such the elements of control and empowerment are reduced. The daughter here may learn to subvert the system but this story does not necessarily emphasise the principles of choice and control and the partnership of care (DoH, 1993).

The third and final strand of this analysis focuses on the concept of intergenerational connectedness. Here the stories told see women as doers and knowers. The powerful and creative force of birth is acknowledged and women value their own strengths passing on a powerful birth message to their daughters. The active participation of women in their own birth and the partnership of care principle which enshrines and recognises the validity of women's experiences and this is the legacy that is passed on to their daughters.

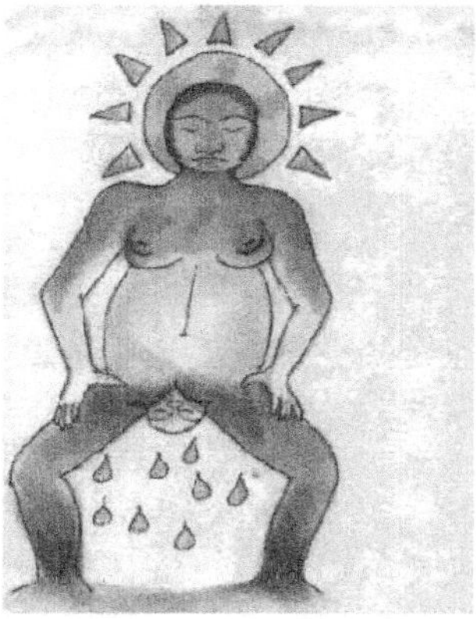

Rainbow Woman Gives Birth to Water Baby; drawn by a 38 year old woman and her 7 year old daughter to describe how the daughter was born. Taken from their birth-stories.

In the above extract the daughter and mother have used visual imagery to record part of their birth stories. The message conveyed by this image is in sharp contrast to the first extract recorded, where the woman was in passive receipt of care. Here birth is portrayed as a powerful and creative process, and it can be argued that the daughter in this example has received birth knowledge that is empowering and positive. However, this form of knowledge transmission is neither detached, objective or scientific. There is a strong element of personal strength in these stories. The strengths of the individual women shine through the stories they tell, and this in turn is reflected in the daughters' accounts of the stories.

I think my Mummy was very clever because first of all she had me and then she went and got me a brother - the midwife said she was clever too!

Eight-year old girl retelling part of a family birth story. Birth stories represent a powerful yet little utilised source of knowledge. In England, where women and midwives struggle to ensure that birth remains a spiritual and psycho-physiological event, using birth stories and recognising the knowledge contained within them is one way of passing birth wisdom down through the generations. We are in danger of having intervention and its accompanying abnormalities perceived as our cultural norm and powerful birth as the deviation. If this happens we will become spiritually and culturally impoverished; birth will truly have been transformed into a process that needs to be regulated and controlled. We will then have Jost the valuable knowledge and wisdom of generations of women.

Mothers who have fears also hand down fearful attitudes about births to daughters - and to every other woman who will listen. But each woman who gains the confluence to birth unhindered or as freely as her biological circumstances will allow- she will go on to encourage her sisters and daughters with birth words and images that resound with all the potential strength and beauty of birth. (Tritten, 1995)

REFERENCES

Cominsky , S (1982).'Childbirth and change: A Guatemalan study', 205- 229, in: Maccormack CP (ed), *Ethnography of Fertility and Birth*; Academic Press, London.

Van Gennep, A (1909). *Rites of Passage*, Routledge and Kegau Paul / London.

Marshall, H (1993). 'The social construction of motherhood: An analysis of child care and parenting anuals' 66-85, in: PhoenixA, Woollett A and Lloyd E (eds), *Motherhood, Meanings, Practices and Ideologies*, Sage,London.

Bourne, G (1979). *Pregnancy*, Pan, London.

McHugh,N (1 993). 'Bumpsadaisy: Images of women in antenatal clinic literature', paper presented to 41 lnternational Conferenceof the Society for Reproductive and Infant Psychology, Trinity College,Dublin.

Fox-Keller, E(l985). *Reflections on Gender and Science*, Yale University Press, New Haven.

Field Belenky M, McVicker Clinchy B, RuleGoldberger N and MaltuckTarule J (1997) (2nd edn). *Women's Ways of Knowing*, Basic Books, New York.

Department of Health (1993). *Changing Childbirth: Report of the Expert Maternity Group*, HMSO, London

Tritten, J (1997). 'Making the new way', Extract from Issue 19 *Midwifery Today*.

Midwifery Matters 89

TRUST

Midwife Voice

U - A midwife member from Canada's written contribution - *'I also like to think my role is to start discussions with pregnant people at the first visit about trusting their bodies, believing they can deliver this baby vaginally, are growing a baby to suit their body size and shape. I encourage self-education too about exercises to support the best balance of the pelvis, health and ability to deliver the baby vaginally. Of course, I also must present the low chance that their birth may become high risk and interventions may be needed for safety. Yet I always go back to... "if the risk of X is 2%, remember there is a 98% chance it will go right!"'*

Midwife Voice

P - A long-time ARM member - *'...I feel very nervous to talk, but it's wonderful to get together and share - caring and sharing – yeah, this is what we would do every ARM meeting. I still often do the holding thing for 'caring and sharing'. It's been just great, hearing different peoples' bits, and I've made a few notes, so I might not look at you when I'm talking so much, 'cause I want to just include the different things that I've written down sort of, and I really like C**** talking about being true to herself. And I think sort of, yeah, my words about being authentic and trying to be as authentic and something about being radical, about being alive, staying alive, and living on that edge of... like the quick, and the sort of, Cambian... be alive... edge... the living edge. So the growing edge, as well the edge that is sort of sensitive. So for me, it's been about being in tune, and intuitive, about tuning in to what's happening, being with women and about touching... touching the earth, being in touch with the earth. In, sort* *of, Buddhist practise, touching the earth - of the roots - the origins - the earth - the dirt - the ground of our being. It's been really important to me'*

A Birth Story

So what birth do I consider the 'highest risk' I ever attended? I'm not 100% certain, but this next one could be a contender - A VBAC of twins, presenting double breech. This was one of my early twin cases, when I still needed the support of my mentor, Mary Cronk, and as always, we followed Mary's own 'guidelines', ensuring that we had enough pairs of hands available at the birth for any emergency - essentially, a minimum of three midwives, one for mum, and one for each baby. In the event, we also had a student midwife, and with the family we had a delightfully full birth room, with the dad, two other children and a granny.

Bridget spontaneously went into labour significantly past her due date, seen as highly unusual in obstetric circles. Twins are said to arrive early owing to a variety of theories - lack of space, failing placentae and so on. None proved as far as I know. In my experience, twins quite regularly got to term and beyond. Talking with Mary, we had concluded that women who had 'normal' midwifery care, without the harum-scarum of obstetric monitoring and fear-based input, remained relaxed allowing labour to proceed when the babies saw fit. What we did know about Bridget's pregnancy, an instant reassurance, was these were dizygotic twins - the most uneventful twin pregnancy statistically having all their own environment - two of everything, amnion, chorion and placentae. So we weren't unduly concerned when both decided to present breech at term.

Bridget had an impressive girth, and we were satisfied that the babies were growing well. The day of labour arrived, and the first baby, a girl, arrived bottom first without incident, a respectable weight nearly 7lbs. This was the day that I learned how important, and useful, an upright, active labouring woman was with twins, instead of the hospital recommendation of epidural, closely monitored and confined to a bed. Bridget wandered around, didn't lay down at all until both babies were born, even though we had quite a wait on our hands for the second twin... nearly two hours before she began to spontaneously push again. Previously, I had observed, that instead of babies popping out in quick succession, it was more usual for women to be given time by nature to observe, feed, nurture the first born for a considerable period before having to get down to the business of birthing again.

Bridget had to work hard in the end to birth the second baby - very hard. We even got out the birth stool - she was very tired, not surprisingly, by this time. The baby seemed to be taking rather a long time to become visible at the introitus, and we were considering offering a VE, but the FH was strong and regular, and the baby remained a longitudinal lie. We couldn't be certain of intact membranes, but just when we were thinking that we may have to 'enquire into her case' (a term used centuries ago by midwives instead of VE - vaginal examination - I love it), we saw the tip of something... I say something - it wasn't a bare bottom or a foot. It was the vertex of a nicely hairy head. The baby had taken a while, but Mary deduced that in the void of space left by the first-born twin, floated around a bit before gravity took over, the heaviest part, the head, taking up residence in the brim of the pelvis, enabled by an active and upright labouring woman. But why so long to negotiate the birth canal?

I'll put you out of your misery quickly - we had to wait a while. A long second stage by multip (woman who'd had a baby before) standards, let alone twins. No hold ups, just slow... because *he* was bigger than his sister - quite a bit bigger - close to 9lbs! That's what you call well grown twins - and along with two placentae and fluid, no wonder Bridget was gloriously huge. What a woman. Confident and trusting in her body, trusting in her midwives, and the feeling was mutual. Twins can be 'normal'.

Coven contribution

To me being 'radical' is about being the sort of midwife who adheres to the principles of midwifery which holds the woman at the centre of her care.

I have been a member of ARM since 1980. In those days I took active part in the organisation I felt most in tune with, for its ethos of working at the 'root' or 'fundamental nature' of midwifery, and its impacts on societies.

I am very proud of being 'radical' and think the concept is critical to me in maintaining/sustaining the concepts and practices which benefit women and their childbearing.

This concept helps to keep me keen for good practice, excites my passion for research and refreshing evidence for practice in the challenging world of the neoliberalism which has infected our wonderful profession.

Elsie Gayle

A Birth Story - Post Dates

Many of the stories of birth that I share, begin with a desperate woman. As an Independent Midwife working outside of the NHS, I was known to take on clients who challenged medical advice. A common such scenario (and sadly one that has increased in recent years) concerns the recommendation for induction of labour (IOL) post dates. I used to blithely contend that *'all apples don't fall from the tree at the same time'*, reassuring women that whilst the average range for a spontaneous labour was 37-42 weeks of pregnancy, there were still others that may labour before and after these times and still be considered normal.

Amy called me one humid summer's day, to enquire if I'd be

available for her birth - *"...anytime now?"* A midwife at the antenatal clinic in the hospital had surreptitiously handed Amy my phone number, clearly desperately sorry for the young woman. I used to work at that hospital and as the midwives knew me, it wasn't unusual for some of them to pass my details to women - women whose requests for their labour and births challenged the NHS policies and guidelines - women who had fallen out with doctors over *declining their advice* - women who were at their wit's end.

"Anytime now? When are you due?" I asked.

"I'm 18 days past my due date...." She then went on to describe that since she'd 'refused' (the hospital's word) induction at 41 weeks for post dates, she'd had to attend the antenatal clinic every day for monitoring; a CTG (cardiotocograph – recording on paper of the foetal heart) trace daily to check the foetal heart. Without getting into the entire subject of IOL or CTG technology, both of which are not backed by sound research (whole books have been written about this) Amy had sat in the clinic, a stuffy, noisy, busy hospital ward, waiting until they could 'fit her in' for almost two weeks - sometimes a wait of 2-3 hours. Occasionally a kindly midwife or care assistant would offer her a cuppa. If that isn't 'punishment', what is? I was appalled, but not that surprised. A long conversation ensued.

What struck me, was that this was not an angry, tearful, or dramatic exchange. Rather I listened, whilst a woman expressed her belief in her body, that labour would come when the baby was ready; she owned animals and worked in the natural world - she trusted nature. That would be enough for me at any time - but for the record, she was educated, articulate and rather than the demeanour of a desperate woman, she came across as simply exhausted. For more than ten days, she had attended the clinic and each day a doctor, on seeing a 'healthy trace' on the CTG, turned the screws a bit more, as she and the baby defied them, the shroud waving becoming ever more blatant.

"Your baby is twice as likely to be still born if you're not induced..." and other outrageous assertions. *What an amazingly strong woman*, was all I could think, that and *I so want to be your midwife.*

I have no doubt, that had Amy not been bullied, her relaxed attitude towards all things natural would have meant a labour earlier than this 18 day, post dates scenario - but the stress of the situation, meant that she was no longer relaxed and certainly no longer trusted her carers. It's not actually that simple taking on a woman who does not trust medical and midwifery staff. I knew that I would need to spend a lot of time with her to gain her trust, just as she did with the various waifs and stray animals that she cared for. I committed to see her every day until the baby was born. Yes, I was checking her and her baby's health, but mostly, I was sharing my philosophy of birth, demonstrating how it aligned with her own ideals, and ensuring that she knew that I also trusted her; I knew that if anything was not right, either my checks would show this, or, and this was most important, Amy herself would be aware and alert to any problem. (I could share so many other stories where women 'felt' something was wrong and medical checks did not diagnose a problem, but later, the woman's fears were realised....) I trusted women's intuition on this. A woman is physically and emotionally connected to her baby; all women, in my experience, want what's best for their babies - they do not take risks willy nilly!

A long story short. Yes, Amy went into labour herself twenty - four days after her due date. Not surprisingly, it was a long and difficult labour. She was incredibly strong, labouring for more than a day before the labour just arrested - stopped being effective and the baby's heart was no longer within normal limits. We transferred into the very same hospital that had caused so much conflict for her, but in those days, I had an honorary contract and was able to continue her care as we consulted with the doctors. Some births need help. (I've always loved the simplicity of this phrase, taught to me by Mary Cronk). Amy accepted the acceleration of labour with drugs, but on her terms, in her own time, and was helped again just at the end with an assisted delivery by a doctor.

This was not a failed home birth. It was necessary intervention in the woman's eyes. The baby was born, healthy and Amy and her husband took her home, that same day. The key was that, in the end at least, the woman had come to terms with her experience.

Hindsight is a wonderful thing. Just to say, the next time Amy was pregnant, she booked me right at the beginning of pregnancy, and went on to have a beautiful home, water birth.

Midwife Voice

J - Midwife - *'...I was told that I was far too obsessed with normal. The day that I got marked, got the final birth I attended, my 40th, that I need ticked off, the consultant obstetrician said to me, "are you taking blah blah room?" and I said "yes, I'm going to see..." (the woman's name) and he said, "go normalise her." [laughs] So I kind of managed to show people, that by supporting the tiniest little bits of the humanity, and the love, and the normalness, and we can make a huge difference...'*

Article

Moral Injury - an introduction for Midwives

I stand rooted to the spot and just stare at the scene before me. The woman is struggling against the staff as she is pushed onto the bed and her legs are pulled into the stirrups. I want to step forward and stop them, but I do not. She's already crying out in pain and I know why. How can they miss the massive scars almost the full length of her legs, both sides the result of extensive hip surgery?

"Please don't" she begs through her tears, "it hurts my hips." My eyes sting, and I consciously adopt my well-practised professional face, blank, emotionless, it is a real effort, but I've had lots of practice now.

It's all my fault, as it was I who called for assistance. There she was, labouring beautifully, a primip progressing so fast that I believed her to be fully dilated in less than 2 hours. Usually I'd just let them push, the old trick, doing good by stealth; confirm full dilatation when the vertex is visible as this gives a woman much more time for second stage. But today I have a student with me and I should do things *properly*. So when my offer of a vaginal examination is accepted, I go ahead, hopeful that she will progress through second stage as rapidly.

There's my first mistake; instead of simply the confirmation of full dilatation, which she is, I discover it's a breech. Undiagnosed, I took over her care after she transferred from the ward in labour. My second mistake, I follow 'the guidelines' and press the emergency bell; I must be a good example for this student. I have only been qualified a couple of years and do not yet have the confidence to share my true philosophy with everyone I work with. Any controversial challenge of practice guidelines could make things complicated for a student, I believed then.

This was just weeks before I left hospital midwifery practice forever. A rather fortuitous course of events meant that I was able to second to a private birth centre covering a maternity leave before moving on to community midwifery in another Trust. Fortunate indeed, as if I'd stayed, it was always going to be a choice between my health and wellbeing, or my career.

What I did not know at the time, was that I was accumulating experiences that were contributing to a form of Post Traumatic Stress Disorder (PTSD) that I now realise, never really left my practice completely. Years later, as an independent midwife, every time I entered a hospital I felt the creeping fear and panic of those early experiences. By this time, though, I had really mastered the professional facade, my armour was strong.

A lot has been written about PTSD and birth, but the vast majority is from the woman's perspective rather than the midwife's. I've met a lot of traumatised midwives in my time, and most of us, were woefully ignorant of our damage.

Recently I came across the term 'moral injury', and immediately I understood why I had suffered, in silence, whilst working within the NHS. This term has been used mostly with regard to war and conflict, referring to soldiers and why they suffer post-traumatic stress. It is not always simply a case of witnessing horror, it is knowing that you are complicit in a situation that causes harm, or part of a group causing harm that is completely at odds with your own philosophy. What a perfect description of how I felt that day on labour ward, and so many other times. The description in relation to soldiers is often described as "perpetrating, failing to prevent, bearing witness to, or learning about acts that transgress deeply held moral beliefs and expectations." It has even been said that it is "a deep soul wound that pierces a person's identity, sense of morality, and relationship to society." That is it exactly. That is what I felt, too often, working within the NHS as a midwife.

One of the problems is recognising moral injury, as the condition was pertinent in relation only to soldiers initially. When it came to health workers, the term burnout has been more often, erroneously applied. Most of us are quite familiar with burnout, and the collection of symptoms associated with it. Indeed today, I'm certain that most midwives suffer one or more of these in their work, at least some of the time such as: cynicism, decreased productivity, exhaustion.

Midwives stay in the system as they are committed. They have a 'calling', a vocation to be a midwife, and have come through a challenging training often involving debt, sacrifice, and guilt. I reminded myself of my own journey in researching this article by reading my 'Diary of a Student Midwife' which was published regularly in the early 1990's in the NCT magazine New Generation. I'd forgotten much. It wasn't unusual for me to drive over 100 miles to deposit children at a grandparent in the holidays before going on a shift. I described shifts ending in tears, the stress of completing a course that demanded 100% attendance in lectures and shifts; if sick, we had learning contracts to complete for theory and spent days off working to make up time. To suggest that any midwife is not 'resilient' is insulting, I believe.

Back in 2003, Jenny Hall wrote a comment in The Practising Midwife (TPM) about an aspect of moral injury without using the term, but her words clearly recognise this problem. In 'Examinations and assault - what is going on?' (TPM, 6 (7) page 4) Jenny raises a very serious issue that seemed to be on the increase concerning abuse of women during vaginal examinations. Today in the USA they sometimes use the term 'birth rape'; a shocking description. Horrific as this is, sometimes the onlookers are forgotten in the argument. Jenny questions in her piece about the power relationship over such observers, why they do not act, and the knock-on effect. Moral injury is a good place to start, to question, and move on to solutions. I have observed, that once a 'condition' is recognised, given a name, people begin to take it seriously, at least in the world of medicine.

During the preparation of this article, an excellent feature on a piece of research was published in the AIMS journal (2019, Patterson J, Vol 30, No 4). The title, 'Traumatised Midwives; Traumatised Women' caught my attention. The focus of the article is how women and midwives respond to PTSD and goes someway to explaining why a damaging and judgemental culture grows, as Patterson identifies that *". . . witnessing women experiencing potentially traumatic birth events may compromise midwives' abilities to maintain positive interactions with women."* Essentially, midwives adapt their behaviour as a form of survival within the toxic environment of many NHS maternity services changing from offering a midwifery model of 'Care as Gift' to a medicalised model of 'Vigil of Care'. Burnout is identified and belief in the birth process is eroded as midwives modify their actions enabling them to stay within their job, but leaves them struggling for any satisfaction in their role. This is where the word *resilience* becomes fashionable. It is bandied around like a badge of honour, that only worthwhile midwives earn, the ones *not* breaking down. This is at best, unfair, at worst, bullying. What is starting to be realised is that burnout in itself, is a symptom of an increasingly broken healthcare system and Patterson is clear where the responsibility lies.

What I found particularly interesting is that what Patterson discusses, includes an element of Moral Injury, I believe, although it is not specified. The nearest was a 'Take home point' that " . . . *conflict between models of midwifery care and working within toxic culture* . . ." can lead to Secondary Traumatic Stress (STS). I was left wondering if Moral Injury appears in her PhD research at all? STS is what Patterson identifies midwives experiencing, a normal response to witnessing trauma. I have concluded that the difference between STS and Moral Injury is the resistance to modifying behaviour from a midwifery model to a medicalised model, either intentionally or by virtue of inability to change. And thank goodness for that, as to 'give in' or adapt, according to Patterson means midwives, " . . . *may suppress their emotions and present a hardened demeanour* . . ." , so I am thankful that I did not 'only' experience STS. The silver lining though, is perhaps that women and midwives may not be suffering in vain and that by not conforming, by actually leaving the profession an important issue can be acknowledged. Perhaps there is hope that as more research is published, a change in the culture of the NHS can be embraced.

In my opening scenario, despite the horrendous circumstances, at least the outcome was a positive one for the mother and baby. The Registrar on duty was a very experienced obstetrician from Africa who was skilled in breech delivery, and I observed, the kindest practitioner involved, as I involuntarily took on the role of spectator. He simply allowed the woman's body to do the work, speaking softly in encouragement and it was all very fast and efficient in the end. I noted that he expertly guided the baby, mimicking the position it would've taken, had the mother been in the natural position for a breech birth, hands and knees; essentially an 'upside-down breech birth'. Certainly, I have always believed that this experience was instrumental in my later interest in breech births and gaining the skills as a midwife.

Lynn R S Genevieve
Midwifery Matters 161 - Summer 2019

WITCH HUNTS

Midwife Voice

O - A midwife member no longer practicing - '*...so to me, it means being true to myself, and my calling, which was to... is, to serve women... people and their families. The whole witch hunt - it hasn't gone away... it hasn't gone away. Those midwives that continue to support those people in their choices, are still being hunted, and you know, just looking at the reports that have come out, where midwives were blamed for high mortality rates. Yeah, so it's about being grass-roots and fundamental really, in my love of women and people...*'

Autonomy

The birth story I share below, is a part of my (unpublished) memoir, which recounts the kind of thoughts and fears around taking on a woman in a perceived high-risk scenario - just the sort of birth that radical midwives become vulnerable over supporting. If all goes well, the baby born without incident, then fine. But, if you need to transfer in to an NHS hospital trust, then whatever the outcome, you may be pursued, seen as practicing unsafely - or more accurately, practising in a way that cannot be controlled. Daring to practice autonomously as a midwife, is enough for some 'authorities' to see you as a dangerous rebel and so the witch hunt is perpetuated. Radical and confident women have always been mistrusted, the patriarchy naming them 'witch' in times past, and today, much the same characters, midwives assisting women who seek sovereignty of their bodies through their choices in childbirth, are persecuted.

Just like all midwives, I had a life outside of my profession, in my case a family life that was a little more out of the ordinary. I share this story, as it also reveals the complexity of thought we have as midwives; whilst our families come first in our thoughts, often our work as midwives must come first in our actions. The midwife who attended my birth in 1962, a home birth, was the classic 'spinster devoted to her vocation' - Sister Brown was the community midwife in the small village where my family lived. Historically, circles of women who had had babies themselves, with a supportive extended family available for childcare, had been the birth keepers. I suspect that the modern era midwives like Sister Brown, had to make a choice - career or family - as society had changed so drastically, but not enough for equality in the workplace. The changes in the twentieth century in the midwifery profession, control being taken away from midwives, away from women continued, hard choices had to be made. I believe that midwives working today have enormously complicated lives trying to accommodate their calling - they don't have to have a famous member of the family, as I do, for the politics of midwifery to impact their lives significantly - witch hunting pursues all.

A Birth Story - A Breech

I pull into the side of the road, a residential area in Hampstead on the hill, semi parked, the engine ticking over, so that I may concentrate on the phone-call in which I have been engaged for the last ten minutes. It's early evening in winter, cold and crisp, the clarity here on the brow of the hill gives me a perfect view. The cityscape a twinkling wonderland of lights and activity. I am distracted from my conversation by the beauty of such an urban landscape, unusual for me a country girl and I am momentarily struck by the bizarreness of my situation.

I can see my destination, not far away now, a floodlit amphitheatre, awesome really, that I have always thought looks like an alien spacecraft has just landed in the city. The mighty Arsenal Emirates stadium, it's like a scene from a futuristic film, not reality at all. But what is reality these days for me? I think of myself as an ordinary woman. I am an ordinary woman. I have a career and a family, a semi-detached three bedroomed home and Labrador. Right now, I'm in the middle of an urgent professional call, of such import that I will have to find a moment when I get to my destination to make a record of it in my diary. Only a complete account in full detail will suffice in these days of increasing litigation.

And yet, what is my destination tonight? A football ground in the middle of London along with almost 60,000 others. Arsenal are playing in the Champion's League, and I have to get there two hours before kick-off so that I may park in the stadium itself. Every time I drive through the barriers of the adjacent roads waving my pass, I feel a mixture of pride and trepidation. I don't belong here, but my son is playing tonight. Just like when he was ten years old, I will be there to watch and cheer him on, just a different location.

I say that I have a job, but it's far more than that really, being a midwife. It's a vocation and as I am working independently, outside of the NHS, it is all consuming. My role is complicated and exciting enough without being the mother of a top premiership football player, I muse. Tonight's call concerns a woman I have not yet met, but whom is pregnant with her first child, due any day now, and it's a breech; presenting bottom first, not head. Once upon a time this made no difference to midwives. They had the skills and the autonomy for such a situation and no such conversation would take place, it was all part of normal practice. But now, in 2008, I have the skills but autonomy is debatable. I must inform a Supervisor of Midwives (SOM) that I am caring for this woman and it is to her that I am speaking as I gaze towards the alien spacecraft. The world of obstetrics fears this scenario greatly, the breech presenting baby. Having made a hash of it so often, Hospital Trusts are at the mercy of lawyers continually as cases of negligence are pursued when parents are failed by the system.

For now though, I'm distracted by the evening's entertainment, a world-wide spectacle of Champion's league football. The game will be beamed live, throughout the world and people will marvel at the players, at my son, and I will watch as I always have, with utter pride and wonder that I gave birth to such a rare talent. For all that, I will watch as my mind goes over, again and again, the details of the conversation tonight with the SOM, the conversations with the mother involved; have I covered everything? Have I recorded everything in the notes? I have the skills, I have the experience, but there is always doubt. If the birth does not go perfectly with a positive outcome, then I will be pursued. Not by the parents, their trust and knowledge are unimpeachable, but the powers that be, the system of supervision, set up to support midwives and protect the public, which has been abused too many times by my registration body, the Nursing and Midwifery Council (NMC) in my opinion. I have attended enough cases myself to know how vulnerable we are as midwives serving women in these difficult situations.

Always, though, my fear holds another edge; I have a family in the limelight. We live our lives in a fishbowl forever scrutinised by the media. Thankfully, my son is ever the consummate professional. He really never puts a foot wrong. Posh has her 'Golden Balls', I have my 'Mister Perfect', and I am proud that the tabloids have never had any material to flash across their pages other than match reports. Proud that I haven't had to endure a famous son who falls drunkenly out of night clubs or who abuses his position in any way. He really is the ultimate professional, it is not a case of things happening and being covered up.

But what if elements of his life were controversial, not boring, but news-worthy? This is a real fear that lurks. How the press would enjoy finding a flaw in Mister Perfect's life; his mother, the renegade midwife pursued by her professional body. So I am so very careful to engage with the system, not only to protect my clients, but to protect myself and ultimately, my son. Therefore, I write copious notes - every conversation, every phone-call, every interaction, it is all logged in unmitigated detail.

But for now, here I am, on my way to a football match, alone in my car, as I'm on call and at any moment may have to attend this birth. My mobile is always on wherever I am. I have missed family weddings, school sports days, but only once, have been called when at the Arsenal stadium. I've learnt over the years to just carry on. Never put my life on hold, but always, my mobile is on and my equipment is in the boot of the car. That's been my life for years, now. Midwifery first, then family. There is no other way to be 'with woman', the meaning of the word 'midwife'. There will be many weddings and sports days, but each birth is unique and special and demands my full attention, and I gladly give it.

Lynn R S Genevieve 2020
Someone's Mum
(Unpublished memoir)

Article

You Are a Midwife

I am a midwife. I will always be a midwife. I could not not-be a midwife. It is in the very fiber of my being as much as I am a mother, and will always be so. I am nolonger a registered midwife (RM), able to practice, I chose to retire early, but no one can ever take away my training or experience.

As such, I still find it a common occurrence that I manage to bring the conversation around to birth or midwifery even with the most tenuous of links. It's just the way my brain is hard-wired, a part of me, how I define myself and indeed how I am defined by those around me, particularly close family and friends.

So there was I, just last week, sitting with my husband and dad at breakfast listening to them talk 'flying'. That is, 'flying by the seat of your pants' literally; my dad has a small two-seater vintage aircraft that he pilots as a hobby (at the age of 79!). I rarely have anything to contribute to conversations that get so technical at times, but I was intrigued when my dad talked about how he reacts in an emergency.

I do remember particularly with my work as a Supervisor of Midwives, how often incident reporting and associated analysis documentation would cite the aircraft and flying industries as a blueprint for 'best practice', for example, having a 'no blame' culture for getting the best out of a near miss and learning from such cases.

My dad referred to: 'Aviate, Navigate, Communicate', the mantra he has as a pilot when things go wrong in the air. During an emergency he first remembers what he is and what he has been trained to do: he is a pilot – he flies the aircraft; then he ensures he knows where he is, where he is heading; and only then, does he call for help. This is considered the best option for the best outcome.

Immediately I thought of what we are taught to do as midwives first in every emergency situation – 'call for help' – communicate – before anything else we do. I started to mull this over and, using a rare but typical emergency situation midwives are trained to deal with, the unexpected breech, I began to apply the differing responses.

The Professional Midwifery Response

There you are, at a homebirth, and you realise that it's a breech, not the cephalic presentation expected. You do not have a second midwife present yet, but what you do have is a relaxed labouring woman with a supportive partner looking forward to the peak experience about to take place (a peaceful, normal birth) and a heap of emergency midwifery kit, that you never use, but take to every birth 'just in case'.

You can see the bottom and the foot is just about popping out – it's an emergency! Quickly you remember your training

– first 'call for help'. Great! No one will ever criticise you or say it wasn't the best thing to do at that moment – not your colleagues, not the Supervisor of Midwives, not the midwifery managers, not your union or professional body, the CNST, and especially not the NMC. So that's what you do. Simple. But is it really that simple?

To do this in the homebirth situation there are choices and consequences. The moment you initiate this response, everything changes.

If you do 'communicate' – you need to inform the parents what is happening and why you are making this call. You can be as calm as you like, but the very nature of what you are doing is sending the message loud and clear that it is a potentially disastrous situation – dangerous – you cannot manage it alone.

The parents' reaction is likely then to be fearful at best, complete panic at worst. You know this is not helpful, but you must call for help first. You could consider asking the partner to make the emergency call? But there is still the labour ward to be informed to expect you. You have two calls to make not just one. How long is this going to take in reality?

Many of us have been in emergency situations where, with the best will in the world, the emergency calls have taken several minutes that seem like hours. That's when it is straight forward and the systems work as efficiently as they were designed. But what about those times when it isn't so smooth running? I have to say that, unfortunately, this is very common in my own experience; my personal opinion is that calls to the emergency services and then labour ward are likely to take at least five minutes, and perhaps nearer ten.

What are the consequences then?

If you're lucky, it's a straight forward breech, the baby just falls out, cries and there is relief all round. The baby could just fall out, but not cry and you need to assess the need for resuscitation. Are you there, present, able to do this, or do you find yourself 'phone in hand, communicating, waiting for a junior doctor to find a midwife to speak to as labour ward is heaving'?

Perhaps the baby has advanced, the legs are out, but it has stopped at the waist, or perhaps it was all going well until it got to the head? There are numerous possibilities including 'nothing has advanced'. In all these circumstances, there is midwifery work to be done, decisions to be made, real clinical judgements that could be the difference between a good and a catastrophic outcome.

The Aviator's Response

First, be a pilot, do what you have been trained to do, especially in an emergency – pilot – fly the aeroplane. So, first be a midwife. Be 'with woman'. Do what you have been trained to do: facilitate the birth. This may be simply to watch and wait, like so much of a midwife's work, and the baby births spontaneously; cries and you can relax, and continue with your professional decision making. You can decide if you would benefit from further support, and make a call or continue with your professional role alone.

It may be that there is a delay and you have the experience or know-how from years of repeated drills – you need to 'act' – you recognise what to do and get on with it. Whether it is a straight forward resuscitation or a more complicated maneuver to ensure the baby can be born, this is what you have been trained to do. You are a midwife.

'Facilitate – Activate – Communicate'?

I believe that in nearly every emergency with which we are trained to deal, to be first and foremost a midwife could prevent many tragedies.

Using the breech once again as an example, the connotations of innocent mismanagement are numerous; the fear and stress induced by the situation can cause the woman to kick into her mammalian instincts and contractions cease the midwife could either be physically not present making the emergency calls or mentally not aware and the baby become dangerously stuck when a simple act by the midwife, such as ensuring the optimum position of the mother for the birth of a breech could prevent further harm. The list of possible scenarios is long.

Therefore, I contend that we should consider 'midwife, save life' and then communicate (Facilitate – Activate - Communicate). This may include communication to the parents too, as in the case of a breech – a whole other debate: do you tell them it's a bottom not a head presenting?

The perceived best practice of calling for help first may stem from the hospital environment; after all, it is usually just the act of pressing a button or pulling a cord to initiate an emergency call for assistance. It is a whole different ball game in the community – as usual a hospital system has been transferred to the home setting, with possible detrimental outcomes. I could widen the debate by suggesting that even in the hospital environment the best option may also be to first be a midwife?

After all...

'You are a midwife
You are helping at someone else's birth. Do good without show or fuss.
Facilitate what is happening rather than what you think is happening.
If you must lead, lead so the woman is helped, yet still free and in charge.
When the baby is born, the woman will rightly say, "We did it ourselves".

Tao te Ching 5th Century BCE

Lynn R S Genevieve
Midwifery Matters 136 – Spring 2013

A Real Witch Hunt

The fears I have raised here are not merely based on others' experiences. I was subject to investigations of my care frequently - almost as often as I transferred clients into the NHS for help with their births - it was simply par for the course, working as an IM outside of the system. There was no trust, despite IM's undergoing all the same training, registration, professional updating and Supervision of Midwifery as our NHS colleagues - the problem was our autonomy - we could not be controlled. Well, unfortunately there was an element of control via the relentless pursuit of us in these modern day witch hunts, through intimidation, threats and bullying. I cannot say that I wasn't affected, but like most midwives, I shielded my clients from these pressures as much as possible, the stress contributing to burn out, break down - many of us have suffered or left our beloved profession of midwifery because of it. But I'd been taught by the best, Mary Cronk, the quite legendary IM, who had the respect of all. I knew how to 'play the game', support my clients so that their choices were respected, but at the same time, retain a dialogue, a contact with those in influential positions - my way of gaining support and trust to enable me to continue my work. I had found that when managers and doctors got to know me, when I was open about my practice and philosophy, I was less 'a scary radical' and like Mary, this fostered their confidence in me. But it sometimes wasn't enough to protect me, usually following an incident or poor outcome, where the Hospital Trust went into protection mode, and sought a scape goat.

Perhaps the most significant case that demonstrates this during my career, was when after the tragic death of a twin at birth, my colleague and I, following an investigation at local level, were recommended to be referred to the NMC (Nursing and Midwifery Council – the body that holds registrations), with a view to being struck off the register - there were a long list of charges. I knew exactly what this could lead to as I had been an expert witness for the defence of an IM in a case at the NMC previously. It bore no resemblance to the justice of courts of law – with probability of guilt rather than proven evidence enough to end a midwife's career; with no true peers to make the judgement.

Our case was not a home birth of twins. This was a planned hospital labour, my colleague and I had been given contracts to care for the mother with the full support of the maternity department, including obstetricians. We liaised with doctors throughout care, and they were able to examine and discuss options with the mother regularly - it should all have been straight forward, but in the end, it was a case of emergency surgical delivery resulting in an unexpected death. Heart wrenching. During the investigation and all that ensued, my colleague and I continued postnatal care with this mother - it was the hospital staff that she lost faith in.

I was lucky. As I said, I had a certain reputation by this time, and the Local Supervising Authority Midwifery Officer (LSAMO - the only person between us and the NMC and certain striking off of the register), examined the investigation report thoroughly and decided to instigate an independent review - even she could see that this was a witch hunt. I am forever grateful to the independent investigator, a renowned midwife from another area, who interviewed us and other midwives in the Trust, concluding that there were no charges whatsoever to answer to. The fact that the obstetricians closed ranks and refused to co-operate, not giving any statements or attending interviews, despite repeated requests by the independent investigator, gives you an idea of the culture of blame in the NHS. The case was dismissed – but the maternity department and Hospital Trust sought to punish us. So sad, more for the women in the area than me, as the option of having an IM continue care within that hospital was revoked from that time.

This was an enormously frightening and stressful time. Supporting a woman whose baby has died is demanding always, but to do this whilst being accused, is desperately trying. The worst aspect, was having a relationship with the woman that lays you wide open, honest exchanges meaning that you know, that she also knows, that perhaps things could have been different?

Midwife Voice

F - Midwife - *'...to be confident and I mean courageous, but I wouldn't even sound... not even that courageous. I'm somebody that keeps my head down, and has tried not to rock the boat too much, because I'm afraid. And we know that being radical, means being afraid, I think as well, that afraid of... persecution, that what you're saying is different, and challenging the status quo, that is it's challenging the status quo...'*

A Birth Story - Stillbirth

Another case I will share is as tragic, and certainly the low point in my career. I say 'low point', as it was the worst case scenario I could imagine experiencing as a midwife (let alone as a mother), the death of a baby *in labour* - a home birth that was going so well. Most midwives come across baby deaths in their careers from time to time - I always said to student midwives, that as an IM accepting high risk cases for low risk care, this raised the possibility a devastating outcome, just like obstetricians' caseloads. This client was a normal healthy woman having her first baby, with only one risk factor, she was a large woman, so monitoring for things like raised blood pressure, signs of diabetes and growth issues in the baby were standard. She never developed a problem in pregnancy.

However, her labour did not begin ideally, she had a pre-labour rupture of membranes with meconium staining (the baby opened its bowels in the womb). This is sometimes a sign of a problem, but not always. She did not have any further investigations as labour ensued within a couple of days, and appeared to be proceeding well.

Transferring into hospital, with a woman in an ambulance because *'...I can't find the baby's heart... trying to remain optimis-*

tic, as there is a small possibility of the baby being ok - on a large woman it is sometimes difficult to get a good FH assessment with a baby deep in the pelvis - but with the mounting dread of 'knowing' that this isn't actually the case, that your client's baby has died... and only in the last half hour or so'... is that 'low point'. An experience I would never want another midwife to have. It wasn't the investigation afterwards, the essential and welcome examination and scrutiny of my care for the woman and her baby that was the worst part.

In this case, independent midwifery supervisors were brought in to explore and analyse all that went on. Their findings were that although different choices could have been made, none could have guaranteed a different outcome. I was invited to the hospital's 'Adverse Incidents Meeting', to present the case. These are important forums, where practitioners can learn from others' actions, mistakes or otherwise.

Usually, there would be a few doctors with power point presentations to a small room of colleagues, maybe the odd midwifery manager. This time though, when it was shared that there would be *an IM presenting her case (AKA a witch)*, the venue had to be changed to a large conference room. Was I scared? You bet. But I am an experienced presenter and had taught students in university classes, presented at conferences (even the RCM national conference one year), and put on my professional hat, giving them a professional PP performance, that I hoped may change some of their views of IM's as *renegade midwives* (witches!). At the end of the presentation, I asked if there were any questions. Silence. At least they can't disagree with how I gave care, I mused to myself, utterly relieved. Then a voice at the back piped up - I recognised one of the Consultant Obstetricians, "Can I just say, that I think it's awful what choices some women make midwives support...". This was the obstetric equivalent of support for me. I smiled my thanks, the knowledge that obstetricians and radical midwives, *'never the twain will meet'* being heavily reinforced that day. Our philosophy of supporting women's choice not understood at all. I did once come across a doctor at a conference who understood, but he was a GP. He said, "If you truly believe in supporting patient choice, then you must be prepared to support whatever they choose, even if you know it will result in death." That's it. In this heart-breaking case, this didn't directly apply, but the ideology is the same.

Midwife Voice

T - Midwife - *'I came to midwifery because of my, in the main, positive birth experiences. I had learnt a lot about birth by attending active birth classes, and I felt empowered by them, and able to make my own choices and decisions during pregnancy, labour and birth, and postnatally. I became a midwife, because I wanted to share this power - that I felt I had gained and used - with other women and midwives. I wanted everyone to know, that power comes from knowledge, and that it is our duty as midwives, to ensure a woman is enabled to gain this power, if she so wishes it. I wanted every single woman I cared for, to feel that she was involved in the decisions made about herself and her body; that she knew that there is a medical model of birth out there which is presented as 'the norm' and that she may not always (or ever) want to go along with it.'*

Midwife Voice

C - Student midwife - *'...I think it means to be honest. Being radical to me, means to tell the truth in every situation, even if you are a bit unsure about what the truth can be, but just acknowledging your own limits and being very frank. So, I don't know, maybe the very silly example but even if you're a student, just saying "I'm a student and I'm learning," [when] something is asked, maybe simple as that...'*

Midwife Voice

R - Independent midwife, written response to question - *'Women come to see me, after recommendation... I briefly find out a woman's wishes for the pregnancy and birth and give her accurate evidence, researched and anecdotal, in relation to her own situation. I then go through her choices... We are the guardians of every woman's preg-*

nancy and birth, not her manager. All women I see completely get it when I say that pregnancy and birth is an art as well as a science and that we lose the art at our peril...They leave happily prepared to regain their power.'

Independence

In the first year of the new millennium, I was to have my first experience as an independent midwife. Not self-employed, but working outside of the NHS in a private capacity, for the first time since qualification, I was working within an environment where I was making clinical decisions based on what I believed to be best practice and not simply guidelines. Of course I had to share this adventure with my ARM friends via Midwifery Matters.

Article

A Spot of Independence

WITHIN TWO YEARS of qualifying as a midwife, I had reached my lowest ebb. My health was suffering, and I was utterly disillusioned by what I was seeing on a daily basis within the hospital system. I had entered midwifery in my 30s, having birthed three children, comparatively easily. It was very much a calling. I felt that I had sailed through my training and had high hopes for the future. Changing Childbirth (DoH, 1993) was published, and more and more caseload practices were successfully running. Perhaps I was too idealistic; I did not think so. I had been through the system myself, and knew what a difference individual care made to women's experiences and so concentrated on my own practice, happy in the knowledge that I could make a difference.

Having trained in the 1990s, I knew and valued evidence to inform my practice, and frequently gave clinical evidence to back my decisions, when I was challenged by doctors, senior midwives and management. But on a daily basis, constantly justifying why you haven't done an admission trace, why you haven't performed an ARM, why your 'trial of scar' (awful term) is in the pool, the list is endless, it eventually wears you down.

The 'crunch' came after a run of experiences where I felt powerless to act on women's behalf, including; topping up an epidural (heavily) on a woman fully dilated with twins for over four hours as, 'theatre was busy'. I now knew that the system had won - I was justifying my decisions by saying to myself 'if that was how it was done by everyone around me, so it's OK'. This realisation was too much to bear, and an extended period off work ensued. I completely understand now why midwives are leaving the profession. I had heard a wonderful expression I heard at a Midwifery Today conference: "I could not, not be a midwife," and this describes exactly how I feel. So what was the answer for me? What saved me?

As fate would have it, an opportunity to spend a secondment at an independent midwifery birth centre was looming. Of course I had to be interviewed along with other hopefuls, obviously just as fed up with the NHS as I was! But I strongly felt that I would be successful, even though I had to convince the midwives there that a round trip of 110 miles a day would not be too much, I really needed this. And so it was, that a couple of months later, I began my, I believe, life saving foray into the world of independent midwifery. In just three and a half months, I was rejuvenated, positive and enjoying being a midwife again thanks to the incredible support and mentorship of some incredible midwives.

For the first time in ages, I was truly working as a midwife. Sometimes away from home for days, working intensively but with fantastic support from midwives and, dare I say it, wonderful chefs and other essential people who ensured that women and their families actually enjoyed the time around birth.

I had been asked at interview what I expected to get out of

the experience. I recall saying that I wished to finally learn some 'real midwifery skills', not the extended roles seen as an advantage in the hospital setting such as epidural top-ups, scrubbing for sections etc, but skills I would need in homebirths, for instance.

This was realised many times over, even in such a short space of time. I learnt about support, nutrition and a hundred other things, but most of all, I was reminded of what I once knew to be true, that women can birth their own babies, safely, without intervention in most cases, simply by giving the right environment and encouragement. I knew these things deep down, but had been prevented from practising accordingly, so that in the end, I began to doubt them, and I had started to believe in the obstetric views constantly faced with in the hospital environment. Now I had a new confidence, a new lease of life but was I ready and able to go back to the NHS? Yes, but I couldn't stay on the wards, I had to get out into community, something I had striven for constantly before, unsuccessfully, but once again, fate lent a hand and the perfect job just appeared. A community post within one of the few cottage hospital midwifery units left open became available and it was only 12 miles from home!

A year later, I am happier and healthier, and although I would love to work independently, I relish being able to offer women midwifery care and not obstetric care within the NHS. In a unit that has less than 100 births a year, I have managed to catch more babies than when I worked on delivery suite! So, to everyone out there unhappy at work, don't give up, women need midwives like us, your turning point could be just around the comer.

Lynn Walcott
Midwifery Matters 87

Midwife Voice

V - Midwife (written response) - '*...Radical midwives are passion-*

ate and won't keep silent when we see change is necessary. Injustice calls us to activism.'

Midwife Voice

I – A long-time ARM member - *'I started my midwifery training in 1981, and I came to it with a real sense of vocation, that this... that I was born to be a midwife. That was very strong feeling for me, and I came to it as a feminist as well, yes, feminist politics in the late seventies early 80s feel so powerful, is such a part of young women's lives. I started in January 81 I think, and after about six weeks, the overwhelming thought I had was, I don't think it's meant to be like this... and that was, you know, birth, everything. And I went to an ARM meeting in Sheffield, and I went away thinking, Oh yes I was right - it's not meant to be like this, and I think that this course, that ARM give me, the language skills, the politics, has just been so important. What ARM's strong emphasis on radical has given me, [is]a link to all, the whole history of midwifery, and on an international scale.*

So instead of being a midwife in the 20th/21st century NHS, it's enabled me to be a midwife out of time, or it gave me that link to my sense of vocation, to my vocational calling, and not just to a job, a set of skills...'

Midwife Voice

N – A long-time ARM member (retired) - *'...that's why I liked that... being a radical midwife... is this sisterhood, and it's sharing of ideas, and the common purpose. I think M**** said it, that as a midwife, that's what you are... you're there for women... you're there for the woman and help to have the best experience possible. And as I've grown older, my daughter's had daughters now, my granddaughters are both pregnant, two are pregnant one's got a child and I just want the best for them as well. I mean one of my granddaughters, she's being shoved down the medicalized path for no reason at all, but my daughter keeps hauling her back, and it's not nice to see. It's almost like it's awful waiting, isn't it, you know, this* *will happen, that will happen, there will be another intervention, and I think that being radical, I think for me, it's mainly about the sisterhood... people who love each other, care for each other, and care for women and ...and* [pause] *then it... it hurts me to think anybody at ARM could... could cause, could hurt people...'*

INCLUSIVITY

Midwife Voice

L – A long-time ARM member no longer practising - '*...I came off birth groups, and midwifery groups on Facebook, because it was painful. To make a transition and a change from having been 30 years as a midwife, to not being a midwife. But somebody said, who was it that said that, you know, 'when somebody's a midwife, always a midwife?' But I haven't really felt like that for three years...* [crying – long silence – more crying]. *But I think about radical, for me, how it felt a bit more tainted, was because of the association of trans exclusionary radical feminism, and the process of being radicalized... to be that. The process happened to many people I know, including midwives. So, then I felt excluded from all midwifery spaces, because of people who had been radicalised into having transphobic ideas, and having to leave long term friends behind, because of their transphobic beliefs, that they had expressed to me, so yeah, my relationship with the word 'radical', has undergone a big transformation, really [pause] But I felt so glad to be back in this space again...*'

Midwife Voice

P – A long-time ARM member - '*...I've been in Birmingham for 30 years as a midwife. I think it was when I went for another interview somewhere else, when I was just toying with maybe I'd go to London, but I ended up in Birmingham, being asked about my weakness. I remember they used to like to ask that question in an interview, and I said something about my powerful sense of being... advocating where there's injustice. Because sometimes it would get me into trouble, when I would be really advocating where there's injustice,* *coz I was very sensitive to that. So like latterly, more recently, I mean, I'm still working, I've always just been trying to find this place, to be involved with home birth and ARM. I was on the steering group back when I was a student midwife, and then, right through, staying in touch. So I've been with the home birth team but just discerning, discernment, where this living place is. So it's sort of, undergone quite a transformation in the last few years and getting alongside women who are not seeing... women and birthing people who are not seen and heard. Stuff about inclusion - I'm really glad A**** is talking about an experience of other people, trans people, black people. So I've been working very closely with communities of inner-city Birmingham. I am managing to still be a midwife, still doing on calls for the home birth team. I think it was M**** mentioning about liminal places, and I think that's what practical midwifery is – it's about occupying those liminal places, and that's what this is about, between birth and death* [pause – crying] *Having one foot in and one foot out, trying to stay stable, and then stepping out of my comfort zone, to be vulnerable. About believing in people believing they are who they say they are, and then yeah, I think the last little bit then. So I think it's actually about being a spiritual activist, right, that's what being radical is. I think that's what ultimately it's all about...'*

Midwife Voice

T – A long-time ARM member (written response) - *'...I have done a lot of political campaigning in my adult life – for the disadvantaged and marginalised, the oppressed and those suffering from injustice. I have talked out against racism and against health professionals who refer to those in our care who may not fit cultural norms, in a negative way. And I have particularly chosen to work with women who may be disadvantaged and marginalised to ensure they receive good care. I think this is also part of what being radical is about. It is about advocating for women when it is difficult for them to do so themselves. I have broken NHS rules – I invited a woman and her baby who were seeking asylum to my house to enable her to have some company; I went late at night to the mother (who was severely disabled) of a woman to inform her that her daughter's baby had* *been stillborn; I have driven women to the hospital in my car; I took a family to the cemetery to visit the grave of their stillborn baby. And many more. All of this I see as radical.*

I have supported women at MSLC, and now MVP meetings to speak up for improvements in maternity care. I have worked alongside women to campaign for... care locally. We campaigned for many years for a stand-alone birth centre – but sadly failed in this.

I constantly post on social media in local midwife group pages about issues that I would like to raise awareness about. (I rarely get any comments but I just carry on regardless!).

I have joined the Working Group for Inclusivity and Diversity as I wish to ensure that ARM is seen as an inclusive organisation which campaigns not only for improving maternity services for all, but particularly for those who are marginalised and disadvantaged. This I see as being radical.'

Midwife Voice

V - Midwife - *'...For me, being a radical midwife manifests in thinking and practice. Firstly it means attempting to understand the root of the problems in birth culture —going deeper, cultivating an approach that enquires beyond what can be easily observed on the surface. So, considering midwifery practice from a human rights perspective, seeking out and actively addressing infringements, coercion and structural iatrogenesis, individualising care for minoritised groups. It means being intentional with my practice, and choosing what to prioritise, listening in for my intuitive midwife voice and not going unthinkingly with the dominant current just because... Inclusivity is a fundamental aspect of being radical - I feel it as a heartfelt imperative, that everyone who gives birth, no matter their gender, sexuality, or ethnic background receives love, compassion and respect from midwives - on a one to one basis, but also collectively, by publicly championing their rights to high quality individualised care...We don't need to choose between celebrating women and including people of all genders. Trans and non-binary people need radical midwifery as much as women, to protect them from unnecessary medicalisation and ensure positive birth experiences.'*

A Birth Story - Mothering The Mother

I found it surprisingly common, to be caring for a client whose mother was no longer living. I reasoned that this was a prime rationale for choosing the guaranteed one-to-one care that I as an Independent Midwife provided, the motherly support of another woman. (Many birth workers will be familiar with the work of Klaus and Kennell (1993) on 'Mothering the Mother', a book that introduced the role of the Doula in supporting women at birth.). This is not the space to debate the pros and cons of this role or the difference between a Doula from a midwife, however, I believe that there are two reasons for the proliferation of Doulas in the west: isolated nuclear families without wider familial support: increased medicalisation of midwifery practice. I think that some women feel that if they were to pay for support, then they may as well pay for the professional support of midwife, a recognised and regulated role, than the help of a Doula whose training and experience was not supervised or controlled.

Meena was only ten weeks pregnant when she booked with me for a home birth. She'd done her homework and knew that she would be able to give birth in peace at home, having had her first baby in a busy city hospital. Her daughter was now nearly 5 years old, and Meena had intended to have her next baby sooner, but soon after Jade's birth, Meena's mother suddenly died. Luckily, Meena's maternal grandmother was nearby, the first generation of her family to make the UK their home and they were very close, Meena talking about her as often as she spoke about her mother to me. There was a huge hole in Meena's life but the grandmother offered a wonderful connection to the family cultural heritage that fulfilled elements that I as a western medical practitioner could never hope to inhabit. One of the important elements for Meena was that her grandmother would provide the support and traditions of the 'mother of the mother' after birth, but not 'at' the birth - the space that Meena's mother would have occupied, at her side in labour, was deliberately vacant I felt, to recognise the loss, but she knew that support other than her husband was vital, hence my employment.

Meena and her husband were both young professionals with thriving careers, and although she came across as confident and well-adjusted after her loss, occasionally the veneer would crack when talking about the impending birth plans as she realised that her mother would never see this child. As I said, I have cared for a fair number of women in this position, so I was prepared for the tsunami of inevitable tears and emotion that would come crashing in after the baby was born, often coinciding with the milk coming in around day three postnatally. But this experience proved to be a little different.

Meena had a fabulous straight forward pregnancy without medical problems and spontaneously laboured at term. As was my professional midwifery style, I felt a closeness to my client but checked any encroaching emotional spills to remain strong. The labour was short and efficient, Meena electing to finally birth in the kitchen - it was the only uncarpeted floor downstairs! Another girl - delight all round; Meena and her husband had not asked the sex of the baby at scan, but it soon became clear that they desired another girl so that they could name her in honour of Meena's mother.

Within moments of the elation, as the baby was named for her grandmother, Meena crumpled - no, she dissolved in the ocean of her tears. Not able to even hold on to her baby, her husband held the child, sitting on the floor, as I made Meena comfortable with cushions.

"The phone! I need the phone - it's over there." I complied with Meena's weeping request, stepping back as I listened, but did not understand the words pouring out of her as she spoke to her grandmother in Hindi between sobs. My eyes stung, and I turned around and concentrated on my notes, a distraction whilst I held myself together. It was only minutes later that the doorbell rang, and I welcomed the great-grandmother to the unusual kitchen scene of a mother laying on the floor, the mess of birth apparent as we were still awaiting the placenta.

Meena reached up to her grandmother, her Hindi words not hiding the pain and loss of her mother in the face of a new life. The grandmother cooed over her, soothing, strong.... I found myself undone, tears spilling as I also reached for the reassurance of her presence. What she must be feeling, I could only imagine - and imagine I did, as I pictured myself in her position; I'd attended my daughter's births - what on earth would it be like to attend her daughter's births... with my daughter gone?

I then watched in awe as this grandmother, calmly took over the kitchen to prepare the traditional foods to ensure a healthy recovery. The placenta arrived now that the Meena was relaxing, and the room filled with glorious aromas as the grandmother cooked. She didn't speak any English and I hadn't met her before, but I held her hands and garbled my thanks and appreciation that I knew I was leaving Meena in good hands. Often, I am around for two to three hours after a birth to support a mother, but I found myself needing to exit as soon as possible - it was the most emotional birth I had ever attended. I said my goodbyes, I would see them the next day, and settled into my car, glad of a longish drive home to cry myself dry.

Midwife Voice

F - Midwife - *'...I've had people say, 'oooh they're a bit radical aren't they?' and going, well actually no, it's just we want autonomous midwifery and good care of the women, the best possible care...informed choice and consent and respecting individuality...*

My Coven Contribution

What does it mean to **me**, to be radical?

I think that I have always been different. Not in a 'special' way or in a neurodiverse way, but for most of my life I have felt that I was going against the current that was carrying everyone else along. My mother called me *contrary*, some saw me as a *rebel*, but what was quite clear by the time I left school to go to Art College in 1979, was that I expressed my *difference* mostly through what I wore. I had been too young to embrace the Hippy era, I did catch the tail end of Punk, and whilst the New Romantics were the trend as I began my Fashion Design training, I revelled in wearing my own creations as well as up-cycled (before it was a thing) second-hand clothes. I was social enough, always had close friends, but didn't ever feel completely comfortable; I think that my, at times, scary clothes (with wild makeup) were literally a *mask* to hide behind. As I said previously, it wasn't until I went to an ARM meeting, that I knew I'd found my people, finally.

Between college and discovering ARM, I married and gave birth three times, the last a home birth. I became a *radical* mother. Not immediately, but after a less than satisfactory first birth and disappointment in not breastfeeding with my first, I found the La Leche League (LLL), a breastfeeding support organisation. Mother to mother support, meetings in each others' homes, these mothers were very nearly 'my tribe', but I still did not feel that I could be completely myself. I did go on to train as one of their leaders (breastfeeding counsellors), which I saw as the first step towards becoming a midwife. I'm not sure that LLL mothers would think of themselves as *radical*, but I believe that the ethos of the organisation certainly fulfils the criteria for this label. In a nutshell, LLL promoted baby led feeding, attachment parenting, as close a breastfeeding relationship that ancient woman may have experienced that can be emulated by a modern mother - that's getting back to roots I'd say, and most people would call this type of parenting pretty radical.

I didn't think twice about the 'radical' label. I was deeply immersed in the politics of birth through the ARM, before I ever encountered the prevailing culture of working in the NHS. From day one as a student midwife (aged 31), that first week in clinical placement, I proudly wore my ARM badge on my uniform. It didn't take long for me to see that my philosophy of birth, my beliefs in midwifery as whole-heartedly meaning 'with woman', were not the party line. I also noticed that midwives on the wards, in the community and even doctors sometimes would comment,

"Oh...you're one of those *radical midwives* then...". I wasn't sure how to answer, I'd smile and nod, but it took me a while to understand that I was viewed with suspicion by those around me. It was a long three years, but my confidence grew and once qualified, I gained confirmation almost daily, that my philosophy of birth as a natural and normal event that rarely required medical intervention was well founded. I have never been confrontational by nature, but the smile and nod, developed into an opportunity to debate a clinical situation, and I relished this - with anyone. Working in the hospital environment we had our own maternity community that included all those involved in the care of women and babies. Discussions were generally light-hearted and respectful...at least in the staff room. After one such fascinating conversation with a junior doctor he professed,

"...I was so scared about coming over to the maternity unit. The nurses in the main hospital had told me that midwives were all lesbians...". Clearly they were having a bit of fun with the poor chap, but even in the 1990s, I couldn't see why it was an issue. One doctor went further after we'd chatted about our respective families,

"...I thought all you *radical midwives* were vegetarian, lesbian, hippies...". He'd spotted my ARM badge and been relieved to find out I was married to a man! Let's hope that doctors are more enlightened today.

This gives an idea of the culture of the NHS that I was working in, once again, finding myself going against the tide of opinion, but this time, I had a whole organisation, the sisterhood that was ARM supporting me. The ARM magazine 'Midwifery Matters', the quarterly national meetings and monthly local meetings of ARM members and like-minded midwives, for the most part, kept me going during my short career within the NHS, but I had aspirations. I'd stated right at the beginning of my midwifery training that one day, I wanted to be an Independent Midwife (IM). I had no idea that they even existed until I was part of ARM, these 'rebel midwives' who were employed directly by the women themselves; they all seemed so knowledgeable, confident and 'free'. Whilst most of the membership then and now is made up of NHS midwives, many IMs were active within the association and I'd been slowly imbibing their seemingly utopian world of birth, where the women made decisions, supported by their known midwives - this was what being 'with woman' meant to me.

I lasted five years in the NHS, hospital, community roles and then a short stint in a private birth centre before fortuitous circumstances gave me the opportunity to embrace my dream of being an IM. It was a huge risk at the time, leaving a regular paid job, with sick pay, holidays and a pension, to become self-employed when I had a mortgage and three children in school. My husband was in a low paid job, I was the main earner by this time. To compound the situation, there was no insurance available to IMs, and it was perceived as a very risky endeavour. It took me about fifteen seconds to make the decision when the private birth centre closed. I could not go back to the NHS, the private sector had given me a taste of independence, working in a natural philosophy of maternity care which was fully supportive. Going independent meant going it alone. In ARM I'd found my tribe, in Independent Midwifery I found my bliss. Here, being *radical* was exactly what it was all about. Finally, I would be able to work with women who were flowing in the same direction as me.

It was during those years as an Independent Midwife, that I learned what it truly was to be radical. It wasn't until these years that I understood how women were short-changed by society, particularly in health care. Being radical for me, means supporting women in their choices, even when it may not be seen as the wisest option, even when doctors and others were bullying, even when husbands and partners were opposed to their choices...even when it went against all I believed in. Being 'with woman', the meaning of the title midwife is the true essence of radical for me. It reflects a need that women still have, post every feminist wave, women never quite seem to gain true parity. Every generation of women has a battle to contend with. At least in the field of birth, it was a woman's world, I felt that women could be powerful together, a sisterhood shared in an incredibly intimate experience. But the Patriarchy hounds us even into this hallowed space, imposing its will and dubious science, the witch hunts never seem to end. Even now, in 2021, all seeking maternity care need midwives; women need this sisterhood to hold on to the sovereignty of their bodies more than ever.

I am now retired and no longer a 'registered midwife', which by law means that I cannot hold this title. *"The title of 'midwife' is protected in law and there is a protected legal function associated with this title. It is an offence for someone to practise as a midwife while not registered, to falsely claim to have a midwifery qualification, or to use the title 'midwife' when not entitled to do so. Only those recorded on the NMC's register as holding a qualification in midwifery may therefore use the protected title of 'midwife'."* (NMC 2021). But, as far as I'm concerned, once a midwife, always a midwife, it is in my heart and soul, defines who I am, but it is the label *radical midwife* that I lay claim to now.

Lynn Rhiannon Selkie Genevieve

When I finally decided that 'enough was enough' and that I needed to choose myself over my passion for midwifery and service to women, I once again shared my feelings with Midwifery Matters readers.

Article

Wasn't I just made for this life? (I could not, not be a midwife)?

This was not my original plan; a grand announcement, but rather I envisaged a gentle fade out. However, I find myself wanting to explain, to friends, colleagues, my ARM sisters why I am leaving the profession of midwifery.

There were such sacrifices in the beginning to become a midwife. My story is a familiar one; married with children I got the calling to become a midwife in my 20's, spent years preparing to apply, waiting for the right time for me and my family, finally ready in 1994 once my youngest was off to school. Vocal from the beginning about my chosen profession, I recorded my training experiences for the NCT magazine, New Generation – 'Diary of a student midwife aged 31 ½' – the first diary of its kind, I believe? An early lesson was not learned (good!) one of my articles provoking the wrath of the local midwife hierarchy, as I dared to criticize the culture of midwifery I was witnessing as a student on labour ward. This was the first time I was 'brought into the office', a little bit of pressure, a hint of bullying, and I wasn't conforming. I was wonderfully ignorant of the power they had over me – I was just a student, not actually one of them.

Strong memories – the training was about making me 'one of them' – I must fit in – it is the only way to survive. I recall vividly in the 2 week break between qualification and starting my first job as a qualified midwife reading Andrea Robertson's book, 'The Midwife Companion'. I cried. I hadn't been taught any of this. I felt woefully inadequate going into that first job, but had a reputation as a confident, capable student, surely this would just transfer into qualification? I suppose it did, to a certain degree. My horror at feeling so ill prepared spurred me on to want experiences that were different to those in my training – to 'teach myself' what I had not been taught – what they had failed to pass on to me. After all, wasn't I just made for this life?

I badgered the managers to put me on delivery suite as soon as possible. But 'the newly qualified need to rotate, for confidence, for experience – I had to wait 9 months – I was so 'full term', so ready by then I had already had the obligatory accidental births on the ward. Pitiful hurried catches as beds were pushed into side rooms. I proudly recorded them in my new birth register. So sorry Cathryn, Louise and Helen, I wasn't really 'your' midwife; I was a bystander, with gloves on. The guilt was complete as you thanked me. This was not what I wanted as a midwife.

My chance came, at last. Delivery suite, 1998, post 'Changing Childbirth' – hope in the air – I could be part of the revolution.

Seven months and 40 births later in my register (many others not recorded, ventouse, forceps and LSCS), how was I doing? Some satisfying experiences; women in alternative birth positions, 'usual' positions I say now. A tentative start to learning about physiological 3rd stage, and a few successes. Once caught without gloves – the 'trial of scar' looking so relaxed bare foot hanging onto her partner's shoulders, barely a groan as baby emerged. Waterbirth, finally achieved, so often thwarted as a student. And then there's the 4 episiotomies that I would never do now. I have done one other since, which I would again repeat, but even that was in 2000.

I was already feeling the pressure of 'being different' as a midwife on labour ward. Every time I wheeled a bed into the corridor, having put the mattress on the floor in the room. Every time I heard the co-ordinator asking 'where's Lynn and her lady?' as we hid in a bathroom with a pinard. I so needed to move to an environment that would welcome my apparent eccentricities. I was lucky; an opportunity to second to a private birth centre arose. I interviewed and was confident I'd get it – wasn't I just made for this life? – 'Independent clinical care but employed' – a perfect compromise – I also knew that, one day, I must be truly 'independent''.

Four months and 5 beautiful births later, I was hooked. I could not remain in the hospital. I had to get out. I had a mortgage, commitments, and debts, 'independent midwifery' was out of the question, but the fates were with me, a community job in another Trust nearby came just in time, only 2 months later. Of course I knew I'd get that job too – wasn't I just made for this life? Fifty plus more births in community later I was just feeling that I'd finally filled in some of the gaps from my training. So many memories – mostly positive, it has to be said. A group of colleagues who respected my 'methods', my differences, on the whole, and a brilliant manager who appreciated my need to be 'on call for my women' and did her best to accommodate this and pay me! During that year and a half, my stats supported my approach – I still treasure that personal audit: 53% born at home or in the stand alone Birth Centre – 83% SVD (spontaneous vaginal deliveries) – 75%breastfed with 85% of those still breastfed at discharge. A personal caseload of over 100 women a year, breaking down to attending around 35 in labour per year with a transfer rate in single figures. But still I wasn't satisfied. Yes, I knew some of these women well, but I was still sharing the care – my caseload was too big to give complete one-to-one care – the private birth centre had spoilt me.

Up steps fate again – this same private birth centre advertised for a permanent midwife. I couldn't get there quick enough – and I knew I'd get the job. Wasn't I just made for this life? A heavenly 5 months and 11 personal client births later, disaster – the centre closed. But actually it was the best thing that ever happened to me. Thirty seconds after being told that it was to close, I'd made my decision to go independent, finally, in 2001 less than 4 years after qualification. At last, I really was made for 'this life' – that of 'independent midwife' – never mind the mortgage and the debts – my wonderfully supportive family had watched when I drank heavily during my time as a hospital midwife, bewildered as to why I stayed in a job that led to such destructive behaviour – they were elated that I found some peace by working outside of the NHS in the birth centre, so when I announced that I'd really had enough – that I could not go back to the pain of NHS midwifery once again, the support continued.

I was so lucky. Fate? Whatever, I know that I had the most dream start of any independent midwife in history (challenge anyone?). With the birth centre closing, all enquiries were diverted to me, as I was the only one of the 6 midwives there not going back to the NHS. An instant caseload. Forget worrying about the mortgage, I could actually start paying off some debts too. In my first year in independence I had 18 clients – and eventually my busiest year (never to be repeated, I was obviously bonkers) with 29 clients! This was, finally, the life I was made for. I attend breech, twins, VBAC, actually VBACC and VBA3Cs, women 'outside the box' – I like being 'inside that box' with them.

So why am I leaving this perfect existence? Well, things are changing, and I don't like the changes. I fear that 'independent midwifery' is in its' death throws, at least, as I believe it to be, as I have experienced it. Let me explain:

In 2001, when I booked an independent client, I was happy to inform the local Supervisor of Midwives that I had a client in her area. A respectful distance between us, we only had contact again if there were 'issues', as I defined them. Now, I still do, as a rule, inform local Supervisors, but it is different. Close tabs are kept, 'support' is offered, discussion is encouraged – my 'outside the box' women require Supervision, apparently – after all, isn't it all about 'Safety of the Public'? Why does this feel so wrong? What am I worried about if my 'care' is competent? There's only one real explanation – I feel 'managed'. Dress it up all you like – but as a competent, experienced practitioner, I do not feel the need to discuss a post dates woman with my Supervisor, for her to recommend an obstetric referral – with a friendly consultant personally picked of course! Why do I feel so threatened? Where is the trust? Am I not able to professionally cover all bases for my client with regard to the difficult decisions they have to make? No, according to Supervision – rather, the Supervision that is on offer. But the problem is oh so much deeper.

In the end it is all about philosophy. My philosophy of birth has grown and developed to embrace all that nature offers, with the rare need for medicine and technology. My philosophy does not believe that it is advantageous to women to have 'all the research', all the information available, from whatever source to enable their decision making. I do not believe that a woman about to bring a new life into the world should be trawling through academic tripe, for the most part, picking through facts and figures, absorbing all that negativity. There is obviously something wrong with my approach – isn't 'informed choice' the new 'Goddess' of midwifery?

*Well, what about the informed choice, to not go anywhere near a hospital – to choose a practitioner who trusts a woman's body, and tries very hard not to intervene, knowing that her very presence is one of the first major interventions? What about the informed choice to accept it when nature doesn't have all the answers and gets it wrong? What about the informed choice that accepts loss, accepts nature? No, I'm not saying never intervene, accept nature whatever the cost – I had a client have a much needed section this year, that needed some gentle persuasion on my part – the last emergency section had been in 2005 for me as an independent. I'm still proud of my stats.

But they count for nothing. So much for science and research. I no longer feel 'independent'. I am checked, and measured, and followed, and questioned – I'm so fed up. It doesn't stop there; my registration body, the NMC, feel the need to investigate the likes of me, independent midwives, on a regular basis. I'm just waiting my turn, now. And the quality of the investigations and decisions I see on some of the cases does not give me any confidence. My kind of midwifery is considered 'misconduct'. I must admit, in print, to not doing vaginal examinations, or maternal observations such as blood pressure checks on normal labouring women. This is a heinous crime, despite not being research informed that is punished most severely – strike that midwife off who does not conform to the obstetric ideal!

I do not feel stressed though – I remember that feeling – this is different; I don't need alcohol this time. I have a wonderful life (many of you are aware, I am blessed in many ways) – I have grandchildren, and yes I was midwife for them, I have a bizarre social life involving film and football people and the privilege of no longer needing to work full-time. I feel I have it all, most of the time. But my freedom, my independence in my working life has eroded just too far – I no longer think it's worth it. If I cannot practice truly independently then I'd just rather not practice at all. Midwifery, as a profession is just not what it used to be. I am so saddened watching some of the new breed of independent midwives coming out of the NHS. I must be truthful, the NHS has seeped into independence. It no longer leaches out for all, as it used to once, surrounded by the sisterhood of independence. It is not their fault; independent midwifery is changing to try and survive. This may be absolutely necessary, but I really mourn for its' passing. I'm just so glad that I was a part of it for a little of its' golden age.

So I intend to just 'fade out'. I now only book previous clients – and the 'odd' breech or twins, there's so few of us with any experience. It could still take a while. I have one client on number 4, planning 10 children – but I suspect I'll be long gone from the profession before then, maybe pushed out?

I always quoted 'I could not, not be a midwife', something I'd heard from an American lay midwife as a student at a Midwifery Today conference, as my absolute mantra. I stand by that. In my heart I will always be a midwife – just not the registered kind, official, within the law, controlled, practising. I feel that I can actually retire, knowing this – it was the last fact for me to find peace in the decision.

The irony is that I thought it was going to be the lack of personal indemnity insurance that was going to be the death of independent midwifery for me. How wrong am I? The life I was made for has gone.

Lynn Walcott (Genevieve)
ARM Blog April 2017
First published in Midwifery Matters 123 - Winter 2009

As I move into more fiction based creative writing, I still cannot resist using midwives and births as my source material. I had a short story published in an anthology, *Stories from Home* (Ed. S. Hehir & H. Barclay – Garmoran 2020) which was reproduced in Midwifery Matters.

The Last of the Selkies

At last, everyone had left. Deborah could relax now, babe beside her snug, suckling away happily. It always surprised her to see so new a life in the world, knowing, able to adapt from that watery world of the womb immediately. She'd seen it many times, mostly at her Granny Grainne's side in the Highland village when she was a girl, but a couple of times she'd accompanied her mother to unexpected home births where they lived near Glasgow; everyone knew where the midwife lived. And now here she was, with her own daughter.

"I must tell you a tale daughter, The Tale of The Selkie Wife, listen well for it ends with a promise..."

*

"Happy birth-day to you, happy birth-day to you, happy birth-day dear Granny Grainne, happy birth-day to you."

"Blow the candles out Granny, then we'll have a slice."

"Come on mum, what are you waiting for?" Morag urged.

"Och lass, it's a grand cake. I was just counting candles. I don't think there's enough?" They all laughed at the impossibility of fitting ninety candles on such a small cake. Granny Grainne blew.

It had been a lovely week, Deborah reflected as her mum drove them both back to Glasgow. Her heart always sank though... going back. Back to the city, back to school, back to the concrete grey streets, bustling with life but drained of vitality, as dead as any grainy newspaper photograph. There were pockets of green; gardens, parks, but this wasn't nature, not for Deborah. Planned, primped, trimmed and tidy, the hand of mans' insistent interference everywhere she looked. Trees stood proud in their false symmetry, hedges and bushes boasted their conformity, every leaf accounted for, even flowers bloomed only in unison. No, that's urban nature, confined and controlled and she wondered if the plants and trees weren't desperate to escape, be themselves, do what they truly wanted. It seemed an impossibility when so many people had expectations of you.

Deborah's thoughts were interrupted.

"Sorry mum. Did you say something?"

"Yes, Deborah. For goodness sake, cheer up, we'll be home soon. I don't know if it's a good thing you staying with Granny Grainne these days. You always mope so. I was saying. We have a new doctor at the surgery. He's only just out of medical school and doing his GP training. He was in the rowing team last year, you know... that race on the Thames every year between Oxford and Cambridge? Anyway, I told him that you'd show him around the town."

"If you like, mum."

"Good, now cheer up...". Deborah went back to her reverie as her mum talked about her week at work. There were always stories to be told, her mum loved working as a midwife, but the stories weren't nearly as interesting as the ones Granny Grainne shared. Granny Grainne reckoned that she had caught over a thousand babies in her time. Imagine that – and all born in homes, not a shiny hospital full of doctors and equipment like her mum had worked in before becoming a community midwife. Deborah never tired of hearing Granny's stories; breeches – babies that came bottom first instead of head, babies born in barns, babies that didn't look right. But it was the women's stories that stood out, their hard lives, nothing but work and babies. Women in labour all week still working on the crofts as the contractions went on and on, tenth babies, fifteenth or more, the secret babies... Once again, she'd heard the story of Maggie, the old spinster who finally bagged a husband at thirty-one years old and went on to have ten children, the birth of the twins in the two roomed croft house the last of her babies. Tiny and wrapped in sheep skins – *if they survive, they survive* – Maggie had said to Granny Grainne in-between puffs on her pipe. She was the only woman Granny ever attended who had more than five babies and they all survived. *God knows what she put in that pipe,* Granny used to say.

"Ah-ha, here she is. Deborah, this is Doctor Stewart."
"Please, call me Peter." Deborah smiled as the smart young man extended his hand.
"Hi," his hand shake was firm, "you'll fit in well with that name. But mum said you're from Surrey?"
"Yes, I'm very English, but my Great Grandfather was a Scot." He had a warm smile and Deborah started to look forward to their afternoon out, a museum, then tea in the park.

Before long, it was evenings out – the theatre or a film, an intimate restaurant. Exams were done and the arguments with her mother over what to study at university were getting monotonous. She hoped that Peter would be a sympathetic ear.
"So what *is* wrong with studying nursing or midwifery? It's a bit of a family tradition so your mum tells me." Oh no, Deborah thought, mum's not recruited him on this campaign too has she?
"I'd love to have been a midwife like my Granny was, you know, in the old days, I just don't want to work in hospitals – it wouldn't feel right." Deborah always felt that she was born in the wrong century. How could anyone understand this, least of all a doctor. Like her mum he'd be totally medicalized in his views – it's the way of healthcare these days she thought sadly.
"You mean like 'the village wise-woman'... *Hubble bubble toil and trouble...*". Deborah scowled at him. "Sorry. Just teasing. Well, there's always herbalism. We had a student from Napier's Uni the other day. I was very impressed, he already had one degree. It's a four year course, not easy." Deborah sat bolt upright, Peter now had her full attention. The rest of the evening whizzed by as

they discussed the possibilities...

*

Happy birth-day to you, happy birth-day to you, happy birth-day dear Peter, happy birth-day to you...."

"I get it," Peter rolled his eyes, "the emphasis on the word *birth*. Your family is obsessed with it." It was the last year of Deborah's course at Napier's University and Peter was virtually a part of the family now. He was a good friend to Deborah and her mother clearly adored him.

"This is for you." Deborah's mum was first to give him a present. She hadn't said anything to Deborah – what on earth had she got him? Peter opened the ornate box and took out a glass object hanging on a piece of rope. Deborah's mother was beaming as Peter held it up turning it this way and that, light glinting, there was something inside. He was stuttering, in his thanks, and Deborah stepped in to save his blushes...

"That's... unusual mum. It's a glass buoy isn't it? I expect you got it as Peter has taken up sailing...?".

"A buoy... oh yes... yes... it's lovely Morag, thank you."

"It's a special one Peter. See inside? That is a caul... a birth caul wrapped around a wooden ball. It's an ancient charm. If you have a caul, you'll never drown."

"You mean that's an actual bag that held a baby in its mother's womb?" Peter was wide-eyed. Deborah could see his brain ticking over; they really are a family of witches... they're using human body parts for spells.

"Wow, mum. You can get anything on E-bay these days can't you? That's a unique gift." Deborah's mum faltered in her smile just as she caught Deborah's eyes and for second looked... what? Guilty? Haunted? It was gone before Deborah could decide.

"Yes... yes... E-bay amazing... it's... it's very old, antique. You must keep it always, you know Peter, for good luck."

"Well, I love it," Peter put her out of her misery, "it's very thoughtful. I will."

*

So much can happen in a year. Deborah had qualified as an herbalist, was just wondering where to gain more experience when Peter proposed to her. She did love him, in a way, there certainly hadn't been anyone else, it was just the way her mother constantly talked as though it was a given that she would marry him that had irked her. This was the only reason why she hadn't said yes immediately. She needed to grow up though, so here she was, now living in West London, Peter a partner in a GP surgery and she had joined a thriving herbalists' practice.

"Oh!" Deborah started and place her hand on her lower abdomen. There it was again. She let out the breath she'd been holding. Not that she needed this confirmation, her mother had told her she was pregnant before she was sure herself, even before she had told Peter. She smiled as her mobile went off – the telltale ring she had to alert her to a call from her mother... how did she know? Always when something happened, she called...

"Hi Mum..." she was cut short by her mother's brusque tones...

"It's Granny..."

Deborah arrived at her mother's house by early evening.

"I'll drive, you'll be too tired... we'll just eat before we go." Morag was already dishing up some dinner. Deborah sat in silence as she picked at the Bolognese. "Come on, Deborah, try and eat. You know what Granny would say - *'eating for two'* – even if it is a load of bunkum."

"Actually mum, it's a very sensible suggestion... if you think of it nutritionally rather than by volume. I do need to up my protein now."

"You're so like your Granny, Deborah. We'll be with her by midnight."

"Mum... mum... it's Morag... I've got Deborah with me." Morag called as they let themselves into the cottage, then whispered to Deborah "She really should be in the care home in town. She's so stubborn."

"Deborah, Deborah... come here lass." Granny Grainne patted the bed. Despite her bright welcome, Deborah could hear in her voice a gravelly tone, and her skin was very yellow.

"I've got you some medicines, Granny..."
"Och, that's kind of you, but I'm way past saving now. I just wanted to see you one last time. Morag – I could do with a cuppa... do you mind?" Morag rolled her eyes and smiled at Deborah before she stepped out of the room. Deborah smiled back, pitying her mother for a moment.
"Now, Deborah, you must listen to me. It's going to sound like the ramblings of an old lady who's lost her mind, but you must heed what I say... and whatever you do... don't tell your mother..."
"Oh Granny, mum and I don't keep secrets..."
"Is that so...? Well, what I have to tell you may change your mind. I won't rest until this is done... listen..."

*

"...so my dear daughter, Granny Grainne told me that the birth caul given to my husband, Peter was my own. Granny had saved it herself after my mum gave birth to me. Carrying on the family tradition to save our first skin, our Selkie skin that held us in our watery world safe, until it is time to choose a husband. Then this precious Selkie skin is given to the man that will keep us as wife as long as he holds this Selkie skin, our first skin.

My promise to you dear daughter, is that your birth caul will never be given to a man of my or anyone else's choosing. It will always belong to you. It is safely buried in Granny Grainne's garden, under a Rowan tree. She gifted the old cottage to me for safe keeping until you are eighteen when it will be yours. A Selkie should always own her skin, own her choices, own her future. We are the last of the Selkies."

The End

Lynn R S Genevieve
Midwifery Matters 166 – Autumn 2020

ACKNOWLEDGEMENTS

First and foremost, thank you John - could any two people love each other more? I promise, the next book will be dedicated to you.

I would like to give thanks to the sisterhood I found in the Association of Radical Midwives without which I am certain I would never have survived midwifery training in 1993, let alone been able to have a fulfilling career until 2011. I am grateful for the friendships that have continued beyond my retirement from midwifery within ARM and also for the support I have received as a regular contributor to Midwifery Matters by the editors. Thank you to the National Co-ordinator Katherine Hales and the Steering Group of ARM for trusting me with the *Voices* from ARM and for their encouragement and help in the putting together of this publication. I will be donating any profits from the sale of this book to ARM, a registered charity.

It all began as a project when I was a student at the University of Glasgow and my thanks go to the MLitt Creative Writing tutors for their guidance and comments on early parts of the manuscript. Thank you, Hollie, my daughter, for casting your keen eye over this work as a proofreader, just one of your many skills as a mother. Having given birth four times at home, you should know how strong you are.

I was delighted that Margaret Jowitt agreed to write the forward to *Midwife Voices* (as I have come to know this book). Your *Voice* has always been valuable to ARM and to me, so many thanks. I may not be a technophobe, but I could not have completed this project without the computer skills of Petra Visser (ARM IT admin) and the help of Sylvia Hehir at Garmoran Publishing in the finishing details - you both have my utter respect for your expertise. Willow Findlay your cover design is adorable and meaningful, I knew I could trust in your creativity.

To all the membership who contributed their *Voices* to this book, I am indebted to you for your honesty and candour - you gave me more than I dared hope. To the *Coven*, I want tell you that your *Voices* are a rare gift, not only for me, but for all midwives out there and I have enormous gratitude for your generosity. And to all the women and others whose stories have been shared in these pages (albeit anonymously) I want to thank you from the bottom of my heart for teaching me so much and for sharing the sacredness of your births and experiences with me.

Last, but not least, I would like to pay tribute to those women (and others) who experienced the true persecution of historic witch hunts. Radical midwives will never forget you...

Lynn Rhiannon Selkie Genevieve
September 2021

COVEN BIOGRAPHIES

Nessa McHugh
I have been a midwife and a member of the ARM for over 30 years. I have practised both in and outside of the NHS and currently work in midwifery education.

Paul Lewis OBE
A midwife academic and clinician for over forty years, I have served on the UKCC, NMC and RCM Councils and until August 2019, was the Chair of Advanced Life Support in Obstetrics (ALSO-UK).

Throughout this time, I have carried a caseload, providing continuity of care to mothers throughout their continuum of pregnancy. While demanding and difficult at times, I have loved every minute of every day where I was able and enabled to practise as a midwife.

I left the NMC register in August 2019 and returned to the NMC Covid 19 Register in March 2020. I am now working with Dorset Healthcare Trust as a Vaccinator but continue to remain in touch with my much loved profession of midwifery.

Joy Horner
Joy Horner is a Childbirth Educator, providing coaching and support for pregnancy, birth and the postnatal period, and is a defender of human rights. She was a registered midwife for 21 years, an independent midwife for 16 years and a registered nurse for 20 years.

Joy believes that the majority of pregnant women and people are able to grow, birth and nurture their babies with minimal medical assistance, and that what many see as assistance is really interference and defence against litigation. She knows that a known and trusted midwife improves health outcomes and satisfaction for midwives, clients, and their babies.

Ishbel Kargar

(After searching her diaries and other personal papers, Ishbel confirmed that she was listed in 1982 as Regional Contact for Merseyside/West Lancs. She knew that the ARM archives would have further details, but handed them over many years ago. Ishbel asked Sally Herbert (who is now retired), to let her know what she could remember. This is her reply, which Ishbel suggested I use as her bio, adding that "she has certainly remembered far more than my 91yr old memory had kept!"

Sally Herbert wrote: "When I first came to ARM you were practically running the whole thing, the records of membership, subscriptions, reminder letters for those who erred.

"You booked the stalls for National Meetings, keeping and ordering the stock when necessary, etc., then driving to those meetings, holding the stall and really being an Ambassador for the organisation. You also took the articles for the magazines, proof read them and altered if necessary. After printing then sat for hours putting them in plastic sleeves and then taking them to the post office for posting!

"All this while being the font of all knowledge the face of ARM so to speak. So basically you did everything that kept it going for years!

"I came along and started helping you and also doing the above whenever you were away. There was also a library of books that was kept, now defunct for a number of years!"

Ishbel added, "Sally's picture brings back memories of an enthusiastic couple of midwives, eager to improve the UK midwifery services. But I am aware that ARM is country-wide, with some overseas input, and that of course other local groups must surely have also had their busy times." (I can only add, that when I joined ARM in 1989, Ishbel *was* ARM...).

Caroline Flint

Caroline Flint has been married to Giles for 57 years, he is an expert on the law appertaining to midwives and midwifery. She advises women having babies and tries to help where she can. Her web page is carolineflintmidwife.com

Katherine Hales

I trained as a midwife nearly 30 years ago becoming interested in caring for women after giving birth to my older children, and training as an NCT Breastfeeding Counsellor. I have worked in hospital and community settings but in recent years have enjoyed working with my community caseload in the North Tyne Valley in rural Northumberland. I worked outside the NHS as an independent midwife for many years which enabled me to experience providing continuity of care to women when this was not easy to facilitate within NHS infrastructure. I was also able to extend my experience of home birth which was the choice of the majority of women in my care. I have been a member of ARM for nearly 30 years and have been National Coordinator for 8 years. My midwifery is from a feminist perspective seeking to facilitate and empower women and girls.

I have seven children and 2 grandchildren with 2 more expected later this year. I also host guests who wish to visit Hadrian's Wall and enjoy the Northumbrian countryside in a peaceful setting.

May 4th 2021.

Rachel Reed

Dr Rachel Reed is a midwife, writer, researcher, educator, and international speaker. Her focus is childbirth physiology, care provider practice, and women's rights (and rites). Rachel co-hosts The Midwives' Cauldron podcast and writes the award-winning blog MidwifeThinking. She is widely published, and her most recent book is Reclaiming Childbirth as a Rite of Passage. Rachel has provided midwifery care for many women and attended births in a wide range of settings and circumstances.

Kerri-Anne Gifford

Active Member of ARM with waxing and waning energies since 1994 and a delegate to ICM for a number of years. Social media contributor and networking activist in order to support home birth, promote midwifery and good midwifery practice and feminism.

Independent midwife in 2000's and founded Notts Independent Midwives Services (NIMS) with partner Andrea Lee. We also founded the Nottingham Home Birth Support Group which continues to this day. Also contributing to books and articles to journals and conducts workshops when asked.

Currently semi-retired and living back in the UK.

Mavis Kirkham

Mavis Kirkham is Midwifery Professor Emerita at Sheffield Hallam University and was a founder member of the Association of Radical Midwives. She worked continuously as a midwife researcher and a clinical midwife for forty years and published widely, retiring from clinical practice in 2015. She is currently collecting freebirthing stories and writing a book on "Birth and Midwifery in an Age of Economics".

Sara Wickham

Dr Sara Wickham is a midwife, speaker, bestselling author and researcher who works independently. She runs online courses for midwives and birth folk, including the popular annual update on birth-related research and thinking, "Gathering in the Knowledge." Sara is the author/editor of fifteen books and 2021 sees the publication of her latest title, Anti-D Explained. She blogs and offers a free monthly newsletter for midwives and birth folk at www.sarawickham.com and she (and sometimes her naughty black cat) are active on Instagram at @drsarawickham

Nicky Grace
I am a midwyfe, writer, hedgewitch, wife and mother. Each day I pray to live as well as I can, to love and be loved by those around me, and to appreciate my life and nature. I am thrilled by firelight, stories, poetry, wild water, birdsong, trees and by connection with people.

Elsie Gayle
Elsie Gayle is a midwife in private practice, with significant national and international experience.

She focusses on delivering 'culturally safe' maternity care; which simply helps any woman to choose services to meet their needs and values.

Dedicated to ameliorate the historical roots of inequalities in service provision, obstetric violence and the poor outcomes for disadvantaged mothers and babies, especially those of African descent.

She initiated 'Midwifery Conversations' to support a wide network of clinicians, students and interested others in the birth world. It facilitates learning, updating clinical and regulatory practices.

Receiving Honorary Fellowship of the University of Wolverhampton, recognised Elsie's contribution, passion and commitment for midwifery, women's rights in childbirth and mental health services within the BME community.

In 2019 Iolanthe 'Jean Davies' Award allowed Elsie to host the first UK, international 'Reproductive Sankofa Conference' to begin the in-depth work of repairing the poor maternity care issues for women of African descent.

Lynn R S Genevieve
Lynn R S Genevieve is a retired Independent Midwife and has been an ARM member since 1989. She completed an MLitt Creative Writing at the University of Glasgow in 2021 and has embarked on a DFA to complete her trilogy *Tales of B-Earth*, a fantasy involving midwives, past, present, and future.

Twitter @LynnRSGeneviev1

...and one day soon... www.selkiewrite.com on Wordpress.

Margaret Jowitt - (forward)
After an idyllic home birth arranged at the last minute through ARM, I began my quest into improving birth by hearing women's voices, listening to women talking about giving birth in different settings, home, midwife unit or hospital, and comparing their accounts of labour and its outcomes from clinical notes. The results were as radical midwives would expect. Of all the variables, perception of control over mind, body and treatment was the most highly significant. No prizes for guessing where women had most control!
Looking for physical reasons, as a psychologist, I surmised that stress hormones might have a detrimental effect on uterine function and so started a 30 year journey into unravelling the mysteries of uterine function. It'll take another 30 years to 'prove' (?confirm) it, but in the end I fitted the bits of the puzzle together to make a 3-D picture of labour whereby the baby and the uterus work closely together to place the baby in the ideal position for travelling through the pelvis. No, the baby isn't a passenger and the uterus provides far more than a downward force.

Meanwhile, I helped midwives' voices to be heard through the pages of Midwifery Matters by being editor for 19 years. I am still a passionate lay member of ARM. I have 4 grown children, live on the Isle of Wight with my cat Tuppence, and celebrated the birth of my first grandchild this year.

BIBLIOGRAPHY

Midwifery Matters (MM) articles:

- A Global Witch Hunt MM 100 – Spring 2004
- Me and my Pinards MM 94 – Autumn 2002
- Too Radical? MM 93 – Summer 2002
- Birth in an American Army Field Hospital MM 57 – Summer 1993
- Let Midwives be Born Again MM137 – Summer 2013
- Labour Pains MM 1 – Summer 1978
- ARM in a Changing World MM 149 – Summer 2016
- All I needed to know about midwifery I learned from Star Trek MM 75 – Winter 1997
- Future Birth MM 160 – Spring 2019
- Comment on OASI MM 165 – Summer 2020
- Story Telling MM 89 – Summer 2001
- Moral Injury MM 161 – Summer 2019
- You are a Midwife MM 136 – Spring 2013
- A Spot of Independence MM 87 – Winter 2000
- Wasn't I just made for this? MM 123 – Winter 2009
- The Last of the Selkies MM 166 – Autumn 2020

Walcott L (1997) Diary of a Student Midwife (series of articles 1994 – 1997) in New Generation (NCT)

Genevieve L R S (2020) The Last of the Selkies *in* Stories from Home (Ed. Hehir S & Barclay H) Garmoran

Genevieve L R S (2020) Birth in the Balance Birth *in* Lifespan Vol 1 Birth – Pure Slush

Wickham S (2021) Anti-D Explained – Birthmoon Creations
Cronk M & Flint C (1989) Community Midwifery – Butterworth-Heinemann
Reed R (2021) Regaining Childbirth as a Rite of Passage – Word Witch Press
Jowitt M (2020) Dynamic Positions in Birth – Pinter & Martin Ltd.
Jowitt M (1993) Childbirth Unmasked – Peter Wooller
Klaus M & Kennell J (1993) Mothering the Mother – Da Capo Press Inc
Donnison J (1988) Midwives and Medical Men: A History of the Struggle for the Control of Childbirth – Heinemann
Ehrenreich B & D English (2010) Witches, Midwives, and Nurses: A History of Women Healers – Feminist Press

[1] Lynn no longer practises clinical midwifery but as she says,"In my heart I will always be a midwife – just not the registered kind" page 12, Walcott, 2019.

Printed in Great Britain
by Amazon

87104727R00122